pelling

and

ronunciation

for

nglish

anguage

earners

Susan Boyer

Practice Book

Boyer Educational Resources 2003

Published by
Boyer Educational Resources
for worldwide distribution.

Phone/fax +61 2 4739 1538
E-mail: boyer@emunet.com.au
Web address: www.boyereducation.com.au

Acknowledgments

I would like to express my thanks to the following people for their contribution to the final presentation of
this book:

Firstly, I would like to thank all the people who trialed the exercises and activities contained in this book
and suggested improvements. In particular, I wish to thank the Bonnello family, Alison Hey, Sheila Addison,
Donovan and Rebecca Jenkins, Jeanette Christian, Timothy Christian, Mark Bagley and Terry Stroble.

I am, of course, particularly indebted to the many students who have given me the necessary insight into
the spelling and pronunciation needs of English language learners around the world.

And last but not least, I want to thank my dear husband, Len, for his encouragement and support
throughout the project, as well as the many hours spent in the production of this resource.

The images used herein were obtained from IMSI's MasterClips Collection,
1895 Francisco Blvd. East, San Rafael, CA 94901-5506, USA.

Boyer, Susan
Spelling and Pronunciation for English Language Learners
ISBN: 1 877074 04 7

1. English language – Spelling – Pronunciation I. Boyer Educational Resources
II Title

421.52

Boyer Educational Resources
PO Box 255, Glenbrook, 2773 Australia,
Phone/Fax +61 2 4739 1538

About this book

When learning a new language it is important to understand the link between the written and spoken form of the language. It is also important to realise that there is more than one way to learn a new skill such as learning a language. For this reason, this book uses a 'multi-sensory' approach to learning English spelling and pronunciation patterns.

A 'multi-sensory' approach means using more than one method to learn and remember something. For example, the approach used in this book encourages use of all the following skills and senses:

- visual - seeing the patterns and relationship between English spelling and pronunciation,

- auditory - hearing words with the same sounds by reading aloud words in rhyming sentences,

- physical - writing the words for consolidation of the patterns by using varied writing activities,

- logical - understanding the patterns of English spelling, such as which letter combinations are possible in English and which never occur in English.

The language activities and dictionary exercises used in this book encourage students to become independent learners and to take responsibility for their ongoing learning. The introductory section provides information and practice in using a dictionary effectively. Throughout the following activities, students are encouraged to check their own dictionary to see the relationship between the pronunciation and spelling of new vocabulary.

The approach used in this book takes into account that repetition is one of the most important elements in learning a new language, particularly when learning and improving spelling. The approach also takes into account that learning happens best when learners enjoy what they are doing. Therefore, the aim has been to provide activities that are varied and interesting, as well as informative.

I sincerely hope you enjoy and benefit from using '*Spelling and Pronunciation for English Language Learners.*'

Susan Boyer

Spelling and Pronunciation for English Language Learners
Contents

Part One

Introduction to the spelling and pronunciation of English

In this section you will:

- learn some basic principles about English spelling and pronunciation

- learn how your dictionary can help you

- have practice using your dictionary to check pronunciation

- learn some basic principles about syllables in words.

Introduction to the spelling and pronunciation of English

It is important, when learning a language, to understand the relationship between the written and spoken forms of the language. This book provides valuable practice in seeing, hearing and understanding the link between written and spoken English.

Some important points to know about English spelling and pronunciation:

• Written English consists of twenty-six <u>letters</u>.

• Spoken English, however, consists of over forty <u>sounds</u>.

• Because there are **more sounds** in spoken English **than letters** in written English, **some English letters represent more than one sound**.

• Each English vowel letter (a, e, i, o, u) can be pronounced as a short sound **and** one or more long sounds. For example, the letter 'a' can represent three common sounds. For example:

  The letter 'a' is pronounced as a short sound in **cat**, **pack**, **hand**, **man**,

  'a' is pronounced as a longer sound in **cake**, **make**, **face** (adding the letter 'e' at the end makes 'a' longer),

  'a' is pronounced as a longer sound in **cart**, **park, hard, are, far**.

• Many written English words follow spelling patterns that you can learn. However, some words don't fit into any pattern and you will have to memorize them.

• Dictionaries and pronunciation textbooks use <u>symbols</u> to represent the different sounds of English. A <u>symbol</u> is a <u>sign</u> used to represent something. For example, the symbol ə is used in dictionaries to represent a short, quiet sound used in many English words.

Practice

As an example, check the word 'welcome' in your dictionary and you will see that the pronunciation of the word '**welcome**' is shown as /'welkəm/. The symbol ə in the word 'welcome', tells the dictionary reader to pronounce the second part of the word more quickly and quietly than the first part of the word. You will learn more about this on page 5.

You can learn more about the pronunciation of English in the book and audio material:
'Understanding English Pronunciation – an integrated practice course'
See final page for details.

You can see all the sound symbols of English on page 98, where the Phonemic Chart of English Sounds shows the sound symbols, along with example words to demonstrate each sound.

If you are not already familiar with all these symbols, don't worry. It is **not necessary to memorize**＊ all the sound symbols of English but it is **very helpful** to understand how <u>your</u> dictionary uses symbols to represent sounds.

＊The word 'memorize' can also be written as 'memorise'.

Revision

1) How many <u>letters</u> are there in written English?   _____

2) How many <u>sounds</u> are used in spoken English?   _____

3) What do dictionaries and pronunciation textbooks
   use to explain the sounds of English letters and words?   _____

You will learn more about how to use your dictionary in the following section.

How your dictionary can help you

Because English spelling and pronunciation can be confusing, it is useful to know how your dictionary can help you. When you check a word in your dictionary, the spelling is shown first, then the pronunciation is generally shown with symbols between two lines / /.

Many English dictionaries use the pronunciation symbols of the **International Phonetic Alphabet** (shown on page 98). However, some dictionaries use different symbols so it is important to know which symbols are used in **your** dictionary.

A Pronunciation Guide (or Pronunciation Key) will usually be within the first few pages of your dictionary (or in the front or back cover).

The next section will provide practice in using your dictionary.

Dictionary Practice

Your dictionary can help you to understand how words are pronounced.

1) Using your dictionary, find the word 'hit' and the word 'heat'.

- Notice the symbol used to show the <u>short vowel sound</u> in *'hit'* and the <u>longer vowel sound</u> in *'heat'*. The pronunciation of words will be shown between lines / /.

- Copy the pronunciation symbols from your dictionary onto the lines below.

Your dictionary symbols ↓   Your dictionary symbols ↓

short vowel sound in h<u>i</u>t = _____   **long** vowel sound in h<u>ea</u>t = _____

2) Sometimes words have the <u>same sound</u> but <u>different spelling</u>.
Using *your dictionary,* find the word *'hard'* and the word *'heart'*.
- Notice the symbol used to show the <u>long vowel sound</u> in *'hard'* and in *'heart'* are the same (though the spelling is different).

- Copy the symbols from your dictionary onto the lines below.

Your dictionary symbols ↓   Your dictionary symbols ↓

long vowel sound in h<u>a</u>rd = _____   **long** vowel sound in h<u>ea</u>rt = _____

Understanding Syllables

- All spoken words are made with *syllables*.

- A syllable is formed by the linking of individual sounds to form **one unit of unbroken sound within a word**.

- A word can contain one or more syllables. For example: <u>a</u> = one syllable; <u>loud</u> = one syllable; <u>a</u> <u>loud</u> = two syllables

- Each syllable generally contains one vowel sound but may contain several consonant sounds.

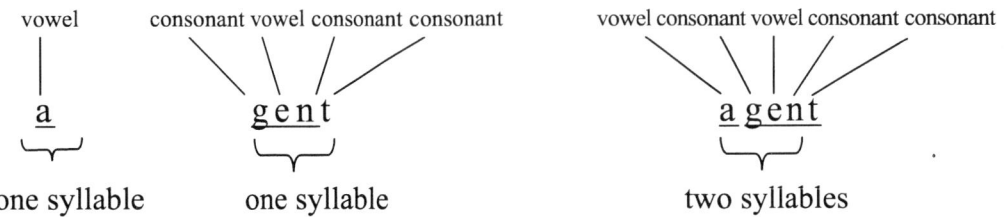

Pronouncing syllables correctly

In words with more than one syllable, one syllable is usually stronger (spoken more clearly) than the other. This is called 'word stress'.

Knowing and using the right stress in words is essential to correct English pronunciation. **Word Stress** refers to the strongest (primary) sound in words of more than one syllable.

How your dictionary shows word stress

A good dictionary will provide very useful information on how to stress words correctly. At the beginning of your dictionary, near the Pronunciation Key, you will see an explanation of how *word stress* is shown in all words listed in the dictionary.

Dictionaries use various symbols or marks to show which syllable should be stressed, so it's important to check which symbol *your* dictionary uses.

For example, in the word '**seven**' (which contains two syllables), the stress is on the first syllable. Look at the way this may be shown in a dictionary.

Some dictionaries show a stress mark **'** *before and above* the stressed syllable.   eg. **'seven**

Some dictionaries show a stress mark **'** *after and above* the stressed syllable.   eg. **sev'en**

Some dictionaries use *a line under* the stressed syllable, to show the stressed part. eg. **se̲ven**

To avoid confusion, always check which symbol *your* dictionary uses.

How does *your* dictionary show that the first syllable is stressed in the word **seven**? _____

Spelling and syllables

When trying to remember the spelling of a word, it can be useful to say the word slowly and picture the syllables as you say the word. For example: con-son-ant; Eng-lish; re-mem-ber.

However, it is important to understand that when we speak at normal speed, not all syllables in English words are pronounced distinctly. Many spoken English words contain unstressed syllables.

In writing, the unstressed sound ə can be represented by any vowel letter. Look at these examples:

In the word **umbrella**, the letter 'a' is unstressed when spoken.

In the word **success**, the letter 'u' is unstressed when spoken.

In the word **second**, the letter 'o' is unstressed when spoken.

Remember! By learning to use your dictionary effectively, you will understand the link between written and spoken words in English more clearly.

There will be more practice with spelling and syllables in Part Four – Spelling in Context.

Glossary of Spelling and Pronunciation terms used in this book

alphabet: The English alphabet consists of **twenty six letters**:
a, b, c, d, e, f, g, h, i, j, k, l, m, n, o, p, q, r, s, t, u, v, w, x, y, z.

These <u>letters</u> are categorised into **vowels**: a, e, i, o, u,
and **consonants**: b, c, d, f, g, h, j, k, l, m, n, p, q, r, s, t, v, w, x, y, z.
(Consonant 'y' can be pronounced as a vowel sound; for example: '<u>gym</u>'.)

sound symbols: Dictionaries use **symbols** to show readers how words should be pronounced. It is helpful to know and understand how <u>your</u> dictionary represents the sounds of English. Pages 3 - 5 provide details about how your dictionary can help you.

The <u>sounds</u> of English are generally divided into two main categories: **vowel** sounds and **consonant** sounds. Because there are <u>more sounds</u> used to speak English than there are letters to write English, additional symbols are needed to represent all the <u>sounds</u> of English.

rhyme: Words that 'rhyme' contain the same sound. For example, the words 't<u>i</u>me', 'w<u>i</u>de', 'h<u>i</u>gh' 'fly' and 'buy' all contain the same sound so we say that they 'rhyme'. (Note: The word 'rhyme' rhymes with the word 'time'.)

syllables: Spoken words are formed with **syllables**. A syllable is formed when individual sounds are pronounced together to form **one unit of unbroken sound within a word**. Each syllable generally contains a vowel sound but may contain several consonant sounds.

A word may contain one or more syllables. For example: in = one syllable
into = two syllables

word stress: In spoken words with more than one syllable, one sound is usually stronger (spoken more clearly) than the other(s). The term, **stressed syllable**, refers to the strongest (primary) sound in words of more than one syllable.

Part Two - Spelling patterns

The vowel letters and sounds of English

In this section you will:

- see and hear the spelling and pronunciation patterns of English vowels

- see the different ways of spelling English vowel sounds

- use your dictionary to learn and understand the pronunciation of new words

- learn some 'rules' you can apply to your spelling

- write the spelling in a 'crossword activity' to reinforce correct spelling

- write some sentences using rhyming words to revise spelling

- read your rhyming sentences to revise your pronunciation.

Vowel sound in the words 'f<u>u</u>n', 's<u>o</u>n', 'c<u>ou</u>sin'

Check the words 'f<u>u</u>n', 's<u>o</u>n', 'c<u>ou</u>sin' in your dictionary.

What symbol does your dictionary use to represent the underlined sound in the words?
The symbol in the International Phonetic Alphabet for the vowel <u>sound</u> in 'f<u>u</u>n' is /ʌ/.

Read the following sentence aloud. Underline the six words with the same vowel sound.

My hungry young brother loves butter and honey.

Check your answer on page 70.

Look at the different ways of spelling this vowel sound.
Add one word from the sentence above to the spelling pattern lists below.

Spelling Lists - Ways of spelling the vowel sound in the word 'f<u>u</u>n'

u	o	ou
s<u>u</u>ch	s<u>o</u>me	tr<u>ou</u>ble
c<u>u</u>lture	m<u>o</u>ney	c<u>ou</u>ntry

Less usual spelling for this sound: fl<u>oo</u>d

Spelling Practice

Complete the following crossword using the clues given.
All the words contain the vowel <u>sound</u> as in 'f<u>u</u>n' but are written with the letters 'u', 'o' or 'ou'.

Across Clues

1) a boy who has the same parents as you
3) people have one on each hand next to the pointing finger
5) opposite to 'old'
7) two together
9) you need this to buy things

11) to rush, move quickly
13) to have to do something
15) ten tens (10 x 10 =   )
17) not too much and not too little but…
19) describes something amusing, makes you laugh

Down Clues

2) problems, difficulty

4) you do this when you want to learn

6) to be nervous about a problem

8) the way you feel when you want to eat

10) public passenger vehicle for road travel

12) place away from the city

14) opposite to 'smooth'

16) a woman who has children

18) opposite to 'go' (somewhere)

20) opposite to 'over'

Check your answers on page 70.

Add any incorrectly written words into your spelling reference list (page86) - making sure you spell the words correctly for future reference.

Make some rhyming sentences using the words from the previous page and the crossword.

_____

_____

Read your sentences aloud to revise the pronunciation and spelling.

Further Practice

If you are working in a class with other students, you can take turns dictating your sentences for other students to write. This will check your pronunciation and spelling!

Remember!
Your dictionary will show which syllable to stress, in words of more than one syllable (see page 5).

Vowel sound in the words 'p<u>i</u>nk', 'typ<u>i</u>cal', 'b<u>ui</u>ld'

Check the words 'p<u>i</u>nk', 'typ<u>i</u>cal', 'b<u>ui</u>ld' in your dictionary.

What symbol does your dictionary use to represent the underlined sound in the above words ? The symbol in the International Phonetic Alphabet for the vowel <u>sound</u> in 'p<u>i</u>nk' is /ɪ/.

Read the following sentence aloud. Underline thirteen words with the same vowel sound.

The pretty children sit and drink milk and the busy women visit the gym in the big pink building.

Check your answers on page 70.

Look at the different ways of spelling the vowel sound /ɪ/. Note that the most common way is with the letter 'i' but there are some exceptions.
Add one word from the sentence above to each of the spelling lists below.

Spelling Lists - Ways of spelling the vowel sound in the word 'pink'

i	y	u & ui	e
c<u>i</u>ty	s<u>y</u>mbol	b<u>u</u>siness g<u>ui</u>lt	<u>E</u>nglish

Note the exceptional way of spelling the sound /ɪ/ in 'w<u>o</u>men'.

Spelling Practice

Complete the following crossword.
All the words contain the vowel sound /ɪ/ but are written with 'i', 'y', 'e', 'u' or 'ui'.

Across Clues

1) a mix of red and white

3) a person who sings

5) the name of language you are studying now

7) opposite meaning to 'big'

9) a construction where people live or work

11) an indoor place for exercise

13) more than one child

15) you do this with your brain

17) easy; not complicated

19) having a lot of things to do

21) opposite meaning to 'start'

Down Clues

2) attractive to look at

4) one more than five

6) the person who wins

8) fast

10) something that can't be explained

12) a thousand thousands

14) there are two of these on your face

16) make; construct

18) wealthy; having a lot of money

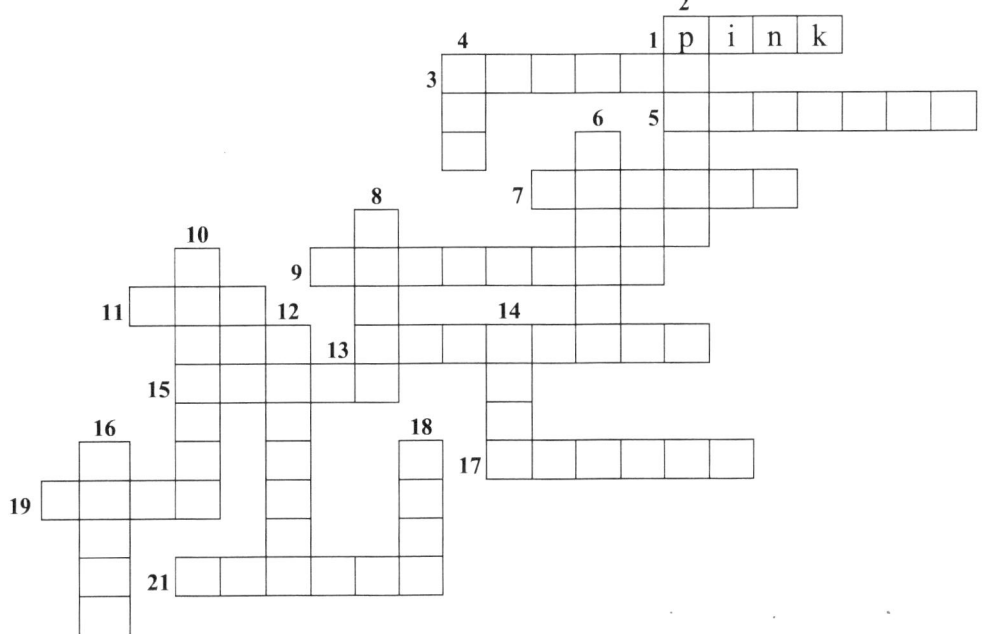

Check your answers on page 70.

Add any incorrectly written words into your spelling reference list (page 86) - making sure you spell the words correctly for future reference.

Make some rhyming sentences using the words from the previous page and the crossword.

_____

_____

Read your sentences aloud to revise the pronunciation and spelling.

Further Practice

If you are working in a class with other students, you can take turns dictating your sentences for other students to write. This will check your pronunciation and spelling!

Remember!
Your dictionary will show which syllable to stress, in words of more than one syllable (see page 5).

Vowel sound in the words 'a̲ny', 'r̲e̲d', 'br̲e̲a̲d'

Check the words 'a̲ny', 'r̲e̲d', 'br̲e̲a̲d' in your dictionary.

What symbol does your dictionary use to represent the underlined sound in the above words?
The symbol in the International Phonetic Alphabet for the vowel s̲o̲und in 'r̲e̲d' is /e/.

Read the following sentence aloud. Underline nine words with the same vowel sound.

Ten guests had many suggestions for better health, wealth and less stress.

Check your answer on page 71.

Look at the different ways of spelling this vowel sound.
Add one word from the sentence above to each of the spelling lists below.

Spelling Lists - Ways of spelling the short vowel sound /e/ in the word 'r̲e̲d'

e	ue	ea	a
r̲e̲d	g̲ue̲ss	r̲e̲ady	a̲ny

Less usual spellings for this sound: fr̲ie̲nd, b̲u̲ry, l̲e̲o̲pard.

Spelling Practice

Complete the following crossword.
All the words contain the same vowel sound but are written with 'e', 'ea', 'a' or 'ue'.

Across Clues

1) the first meal of the day

3) to think about something that happened before

5) the air that comes out of your mouth

7) the part of your body above your neck

9) the boundary line which is furthest from the middle

11) the day before today

13) the person who gives a message

15) to be prepared for something

17) past verb of 'send'

19) to be strong and well

Down Clues

2) the temperature and conditions outside

4) the place where people sleep

6) not ever

8) we make sandwiches with this

10) birds are covered with these

12) two tens

14) very, very good

16) the past verb of 'say'

18) past verb of 'read'

20) opposite meaning to 'begin'

22) a person who has been invited

Check your answers on page 71

Add any incorrectly written words into your spelling reference list (page 87) - making sure you spell the words correctly for future reference.

Make some rhyming sentences using the words from the previous page and the crossword.

_____

_____

Read your sentences aloud to revise the pronunciation and spelling.

Further Practice

If you are working in a class with other students, you can take turns dictating your sentences for other students to write. This will check your pronunciation and spelling!

Remember!
Your dictionary will show which syllable to stress, in words of more than one syllable (see page 5).

Vowel sound in the words 'wh_a_t', 'h_o_t', 'st_o_p'

Check the words 'wh_a_t', 'h_o_t', 'st_o_p' in your dictionary.
What symbol does your dictionary use to represent the underlined sound in the above words?

The symbol in the International Phonetic Alphabet for the vowel _sound_ in 'h_o_t' is /ɒ/ in British English and /ɑ/ in North American English.

Read the following sentence aloud. Underline the seven words with the same vowel sound.

Tom lost his wallet and watch when the shop got robbed.

Check your answers on page 71.

Look at the different ways of spelling this vowel sound.
Note that the most common ways are with the letters 'o' or 'a'.

Add words from the sentence above to the spelling pattern lists below.

Spelling Lists - Ways of spelling the short vowel sound in the word 't_o_p'

o	a
str_o_ng l_o_ng	w_a_nt qu_a_lity

Less usual spelling: kn_ow_ledge, c_o_ugh

Spelling Practice

Complete the crossword below.
All the words contain the same vowel sound but are written with 'o', 'a' or 'ow'.

Across Clues

1) to continue to look at

3) competition

5) something creamy, brown and sweet to eat

7) you must do this when you see a red light

9) a place to keep your money

11) choice

13) past tense of 'is'

15) opposite of 'bottom'

17) this word makes a verb negative

19) information we learn and remember

Down Clues

2) to clean with water

4) a performance/show

6) many; a large number of something

8) a word meaning 'the amount of something'

10) to say you will definitely do something

12) the opposite meaning of 'cold'

14) We can use this word to begin a question.

16) not knowing where you are

18) frequently

20) truthful

Check your answers on page 71.

Add any incorrectly written words into your spelling reference list (page 87) - making sure you spell the words correctly for future reference.

Make some rhyming sentences using the words from the previous page and the crossword.

_____

_____

Read your sentences aloud to revise the pronunciation and spelling.

Further Practice

If you are working in a class with other students, you can take turns dictating your sentences for other students to write. This will check your pronunciation and spelling!

Remember!
Your dictionary will show which syllable to stress, in words of more than one syllable (see page 5).

Vowel sound in the words 'pull', 'could', 'good'

Check the words 'pull', 'could' and 'good' in your dictionary.

What symbol does your dictionary use to represent the underlined sound in the above words? The symbol in the International Phonetic Alphabet for the vowel sound in 'pull' is /ʊ/

Read the following sentence aloud. Underline seven words with the same vowel sound.

The cook book says we should put a full spoon of sugar in the cookies.

One word in the sentence with 'oo', has a different vowel sound to the other words with 'oo'. Which word with 'oo' is pronounced differently?

Check your answers on page 72.

Look at the different ways of spelling this vowel sound.
Note that the most common ways are with the letters 'u', 'oo' or 'ou'.

Add words from the sentence above to the spelling pattern lists below.

Spelling Lists - Ways of spelling the short vowel sound /ʊ/ in the word 'pull'

u	oo	ou
pull	foot	would
push	good	could

Less usual spelling for this sound: woman

Spelling Practice

Complete the crossword below.
All the words contain the same vowel sound but are written with 'u', 'oo' or 'ou'.

Across Clues

1) a person whose job is to sell meat

3) opposite meaning to 'pull'

5) past verb form of 'take'

7) to prepare and heat food before eating it

9) to use your eyes to see something

11) past verb form of 'stand'

13) opposite meaning to 'bad'

15) meaning 'more full'

Down Clues

2) people read these

4) a covering for the head

6) to move or place something somewhere

8) We use this word when giving advice to people.

10) past verb form of 'can'

12) this is at the end of a leg

14) this makes food taste sweet

16) a male cow

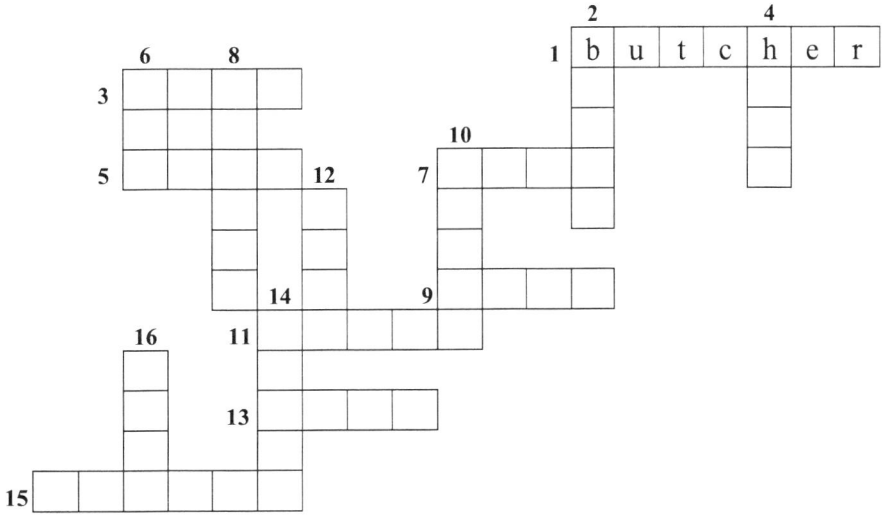

Check your answers on page 72.

Add any incorrectly written words into your spelling reference list (page 88) - making sure you spell the words correctly for future reference.

Make some rhyming sentences using the words from the previous page and the crossword.

_____

_____

Read your sentences aloud to revise the pronunciation and spelling.

Further Practice

If you are working in a class with other students, you can take turns dictating your sentences for other students to write. This will check your pronunciation and spelling!

Remember!
Your dictionary will show which syllable to stress, in words of more than one syllable (see page 5).

Vowel sound in the word 'gr**ee**n', 'l**ea**ves', 'fi**e**ld'

Check the words 'gr**ee**n', 'l**ea**ves', 'fi**e**ld' in your dictionary.

What symbol does your dictionary use to represent the underlined sound in the above words ?
The symbol in the International Phonetic Alphabet for the vowel sound in 'green' is /iː/.

Read the following sentence aloud. Underline the thirteen words with the same vowel sound.

She believes the reason we eat green cheese is easy to see, but he feels she's deceived.

Check your answer on page 72.

Look at the different ways of spelling this vowel sound. The most common spelling is with 'ea' or 'ee' but there are a few less usual ways of spelling this sound.
Add one word from the sentence above to the spelling pattern lists below.

Spelling Lists - Ways of spelling the long vowel sound in the word 'green'

*   A general rule when spelling this sound is:
Put 'i' before 'e', except after 'c'.

ea	ee	e	ie*	ei*	'y' as word ending
l**ea**ve r**ea**ch	s**ee** t**ee**ns	th**e**se **e**qual	p**ie**ce th**ie**ves	rec**ei**pt rec**ei**ve	full**y** Also pronounced as a shorter sound in some varieties of English.

Less usual spelling: mach**i**ne, p**eo**ple

Spelling Practice

Complete the following crossword.
All the words contain the same vowel sound but are written with 'ee', 'e', 'ea', 'ie', 'ei' or 'i'.

Across Clues

1) more than one person

3) you do this with your eyes

5) to take another person's property

7) trees have these

9) under something

11) a part or section of something

13) you have these in your mouth

15) a person who steals

17) a mechanical equipment for doing a job

19) to show something that was covered

Down Clues

2) the opposite meaning to 'war'

4) four periods of a year (winter, spring, summer, autumn)

6) teachers do this

8) opposite meaning to 'most'

10) to get something that was sent or given

12) something to sit on

14) to think something is true

16) the main subject of a book or speech

18) people whose job is to maintain law

20) not difficult

Check your answers on page 72.

Add any incorrectly written words into your spelling reference list (page 88) - making sure you spell the words correctly for future reference.

Make some rhyming sentences using the words from the previous page and the crossword.

Read your sentences aloud to revise the pronunciation and spelling.

Remember!
Your dictionary will show which syllable to stress, in words of more than one syllable (see page 5).

Vowel sound in the word 'move', 'soon', 'rule'

Check the words 'move', 'soon', 'rule' in your dictionary.

What symbol does your dictionary use to represent the underlined sound in the above words ?
The symbol in the International Phonetic Alphabet for the vowel sound in 'soon' is u:

Read the following sentence aloud. Underline the eight words with the same vowel sound.

The school rules about moving computers through rooms will soon be approved.

Check your answer on page 72 .

Look at the different ways of spelling this vowel sound.
Add one word from the sentence above to the spelling pattern lists below (except 'ew').

Spelling Lists - Ways of spelling the long vowel sound u: as in the word 'soon'

oo	u	o	ou	ew
cool	rude	prove	group	flew grew

Less usual ways of spelling of this sound: fruit, shoe

Spelling Practice

Complete the following crossword.
All the words contain the same vowel sound but are written with 'oo', 'o', 'ou' , 'ew', 'ui' or 'u'.

Across Clues

1) one number more than one

3) the answer to a problem

5) to take something away

7) matching jacket and trousers

9) show that something is correct with evidence

11) a few people or things together

13) a law or policy

15) not having good manners, not polite

17) past tense verb of 'fly'

Down Clues

2) the time from lunchtime to evening

4) the opposite meaning of 'from'

6) correct

8) a new branch or stem on a plant

10) to get better

12) allow or agree to something

14) liquid that comes from fruit

16) an area of water for swimming

18) past tense verb of 'grow'

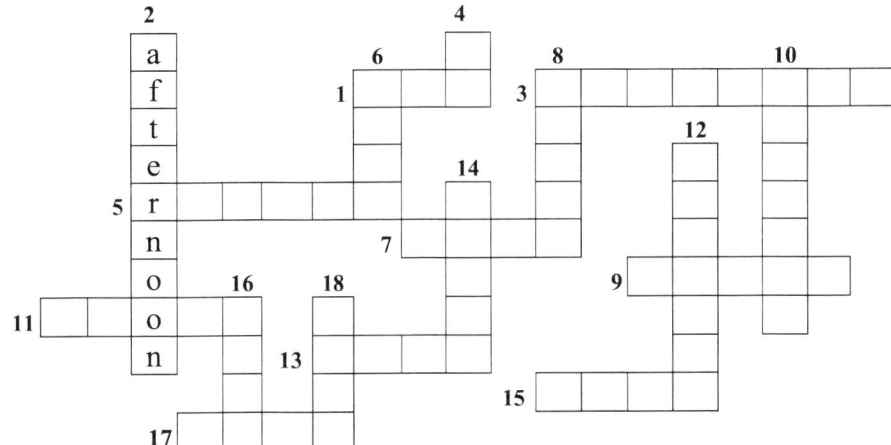

Check your answers on page 72.

Add any incorrectly written words into your spelling reference list (page 89) - making sure you spell the words correctly in your spelling list for future reference.

Make some rhyming sentences using the words from the previous page and the crossword.

_____

_____

Read your sentences aloud to revise the pronunciation and spelling.

Further Practice

If you are working in a class with other students, you can take turns dictating your sentences for other students to write. This will check your pronunciation and spelling!

Remember!
Your dictionary will show which syllable to stress, in words of more than one syllable (see page 5).

Vowel sound in the words 'bi̱rd', 'wo̱rd', 'pu̱rple'

Check the words 'bi̱rd', 'wo̱rd', 'pu̱rple' in your dictionary.

What symbol does your dictionary use to represent the underlined sound in the above words?
The symbol in the International Phonetic Alphabet for the vowel sound in 'purple' is /3:/

Read the following sentence aloud. Underline eight words with the same vowel sound.

Thirty girls in purple skirts will return to work early next term.

Check your answers on page 73.

Look at the different ways of spelling this vowel sound.
Add one word from the sentence above to the spelling pattern lists below

Spelling Lists - Ways of spelling the long vowel sound in the word 'pu̱rple'

ir	er	or	ur	ear
bird	certain	word	turn	learn
first	her	worst	nurse	search

Less usual ways of spelling of this sound: jou̱rney

A note on the pronunciation of the letter 'r'

In some varieties of English (notably North American, Scottish and Irish), the letter 'r' is clearly pronounced wherever it occurs in words, (eg. bird, her, purple) However, in other varieties of English, 'r' is only pronounced when it is followed by a vowel sound (as in 'ar̲ound').

This variation in the pronunciation of English does not interfere with intelligibility between varieties of English, as each form of pronunciation (pronouncing or not pronouncing 'r') is widely known.

Spelling Practice

Complete the crossword below.

All the words contain the same vowel sound but are written with 'ir', 'er', 'or', 'ur', 'our' and 'ear'.

Across Clues

1) the day after Wednesday

3) we use these in sentences

5) study to find new information

7) to get knowledge

9) the planet where we live

11) waiters do this in a restaurant

13) opposite meaning to 'last'

15) opposite meaning to 'best'

17) go back to a place

19) fire does this

Down Clues

2) opposite meaning to 'late'

4) a trip from one place to another place

6) past verb of 'hear'

8) not clean

10) worried

12) to receive payment for work

14) a pronoun used to refer to a woman already mentioned in a conversation

16) a polite form of address for a man

18) to change direction

20) you do this to earn money

22) a piece of clothing covering the top part of the body

Check your answers on page 73.

Add any incorrectly written words into your spelling reference list (page 89) - making sure you spell the words correctly in your spelling list for future reference.

Make some rhyming sentences using the words from the spelling list and crossword.

Read your sentences aloud to revise the pronunciation and spelling.

Vowel sound in the words f<u>our</u>, w<u>ar</u>m, d<u>oo</u>rs

Check the words 'f<u>our</u>', 'w<u>ar</u>m', 'd<u>oo</u>rs' in your dictionary.

What symbol does your dictionary use to represent the underlined sound in the words?
The symbol in the International Phonetic Alphabet for the vowel <u>sound</u> in 'f<u>our</u>' and 'w<u>ar</u>m' is /ɔ:/.

Read the following sentence aloud. Underline the eight words with the same vowel sound.

This morning they warned of four more storms towards the sports courts.

Check your answers on page 73.

Look at the different ways of spelling this vowel sound.
Add words from the sentence above to the spelling pattern lists below.
(*See the note below regarding North American English pronunciation.)

Spelling Lists - Ways of spelling the long vowel sound in the word 'sp<u>or</u>t'

o(r)	ou(r)	a(r)	* a aw au
f<u>or</u>m	c<u>our</u>se	w<u>ar</u>m	call l<u>aw</u> c<u>au</u>ght

---

*Pronunciation note:

Although <u>all</u> the words represented in the spelling lists on this page are shown in all dictionaries as containing the same vowel sound, some speakers of North American English pronounce the vowel sound ɔ: only before the letter 'r', as in words such as 'f<u>or</u>m', c<u>our</u>se and 'w<u>ar</u>m'. In words such as 'c<u>a</u>ll', and 'l<u>aw</u>', these speakers pronounce the sound /ɑ/. For example, the vowel sound in the words 'c<u>a</u>ller' and 'c<u>o</u>llar'; 'c<u>o</u>t' and 'c<u>au</u>ght' sound very similar in the speech of these speakers.

To avoid confusion, the words chosen for the following 'cross-word' activity, are **all** pronounced with the sound /ɔ:/ in **all** varieties of English.

The <u>spelling</u> of the example words, in the spelling list above and the following crossword activity, is the <u>same for all varieties of English</u>.

Spelling Practice

Complete the crossword below.

All words contain the same vowel sound as in '**sp<u>or</u>t**' but are written as 'or', 'ar', 'our', 'oar', 'oor'.

Across Clues

1) the time before twelve noon

3) past verb of 'wear'

5) painful

7) the sound a lion makes

9) the area where tennis is played

11) the number of points won in a game

13) to tell about facts or news

15) tell of danger

17) past verb of 'tear'

19) you usually need to open this before entering a room

Down Clues

2) where two walls of a room meet

4) one more than thirteen

6) opposite meaning to 'after'

8) opposite direction to 'south'

10) opposite meaning to 'cool'

12) this is under your feet when you walk inside

14) one more than three

16) opposite meaning to 'long'

18) very bad weather with rain, thunder or wind

20) fighting between two or more countries

Check your answers on page 73.

Add any incorrectly written words into your spelling reference list (page 90) - making sure you spell the words correctly in your spelling list for your future reference.

Make some rhyming sentences using the words from the spelling list and crossword.

_____

_____

Read your sentences aloud to revise the pronunciation and spelling.

Vowel sound in the words 'v<u>oi</u>ce', 't<u>oy</u>', 's<u>oi</u>l'

Check the words 'v<u>oi</u>ce', 't<u>oy</u>', 's<u>oi</u>l' in your dictionary.

What symbol does your dictionary use to represent the underlined sound in the above words?
The symbol in the International Phonetic Alphabet for the vowel <u>sound</u> in 'v<u>oi</u>ce' is /ɔɪ/

Read the following sentence aloud. Underline six words with the same vowel sound.

The boys avoided being noisy with their toys but it spoilt their enjoyment.

Check your answers on page 74.

Look at the different ways of spelling this vowel sound .
Add one word from the sentence above to each of the spelling pattern lists below.

Spelling Lists - Ways of spelling the short vowel sound in the word 'voice'

oy	oi
empl<u>oy</u>	soil
destr<u>oy</u>	boil

Less usual spelling: l<u>aw</u>yer

Spelling Practice

Complete the crossword below.
All the words contain the same vowel sound but are written with 'oi' or 'oy'.

Across Clues

1) this word means 'containing poison'

3) to show direction with your finger

5) petrol or gasoline is produced from this

7) to stay away from something or someone

9) a loud sound

11) to stop something from being successful

13) something a child plays with

15) work that you are regularly paid to do

Down Clues

2) unhappy because something you expected did not happen

4) plants grow in this

6) a male child

8) metal pieces used for money

10) people go here at least once a day

12) people use this to make speech sounds

14) to get pleasure from something you do

Check your answers on page 74.

Add any incorrectly written words into your spelling reference list (page 90) - making sure you spell the words correctly for future reference.

Make some rhyming sentences using the words from the previous page and the crossword.

Read your sentences aloud to revise the pronunciation and spelling.

Further Practice

If you are working in a class with other students, you can take turns dictating your sentences for other students to write. This will check your pronunciation and spelling!

Remember!
Your dictionary will show which syllable to stress, in words of more than one syllable (see page 5).

Vowel sound in the words 'late', 'weight', 'days'

Check the words 'late', 'weight', 'days' in your dictionary.

What symbol does your dictionary use to represent the underlined sound in the above words?
The symbol in the International Phonetic Alphabet for the vowel sound in eight is /eɪ/

Read the following sentence aloud. Underline the seven words with the same vowel sound.

They stayed and waited in the same place as the train was late.

Check your answers on page 74.

Look at the different ways this vowel sound can be spelled.
Add words from the sentence above to each of the spelling pattern lists below.
(Except 'eight' which is a less usual spelling.)

Spelling Lists - Ways of spelling the vowel sound in the word 'day'

'a' with final silent 'e'	ay	ey	ai
race	day	obey	complain
case	always		

Less usual spelling: great, eight

Spelling Practice

Complete the crossword below.
All the words contain the same vowel sound as in **late**, but are written with 'a', 'ai', 'ay', 'ei'

Across Clues

1) the fifth month of the year (use a capital letter)

3) one more than seven

5) to say someone is responsible for a problem

7) describing the largest or most important thing

9) to move your hand to say goodbye

11) a large area of inland water

13) past verb form of 'make'

15) stay/continue in a particular situation

17) you do this when you finish sleeping

19) where you meet/get on a train or bus

21) verb form of 'safe'

Down Clues

2) one piece of paper in a book, magazine

4) to say you are not happy about something

6) a flat dish for serving food

8) an entertaining activity or sport that people play

10) this hangs from the back of an animal's body

12) past verb form of 'come'

14) the word by which a person is known

16) the number of years a person has lived

18) we listen to music and information with this

20) arriving **after** the expected time

Check your answers on page 74.

Add any incorrectly written words into your spelling reference list (page 91) - making sure you spell the words correctly in your spelling list for future reference.

Make some rhyming sentences using the words from the previous page and the crossword.

_____

_____

Read your sentences aloud to revise the pronunciation and spelling.

Further Practice

If you are working in a class with other students, you can take turns dictating your sentences for other students to write. This will check your pronunciation and spelling!

Remember!
Your dictionary will show which syllable to stress, in words of more than one syllable (see page 5).

Vowel sound in the words 'wh<u>y</u>', 'br<u>igh</u>t', 'wh<u>i</u>te'

Check the words 'wh<u>y</u>', 'br<u>igh</u>t', 'wh<u>i</u>te' in your dictionary.

What symbol does your dictionary use to represent the underlined sound in the above words? The symbol in the International Phonetic Alphabet for the vowel <u>sound</u> in 'dr<u>i</u>ve' is /aɪ/.

Read the following sentence aloud. Underline the twelve words with the same vowel sound.

She likes kind bright smiles, nice white wine, lime ice-cream and flying high in the sky.

Check your answers on page 74.

Look at the different ways of spelling this vowel sound .
Add one word from the sentence above to the spelling pattern lists below

Spelling Lists - Ways of spelling the short vowel sound in the word 'light'

i	i + silent e	y	i + gh
child	time	why	fight
mind	hide	try	sigh
See the explanation of silent 'e', page 36.			

Less usual spelling: <u>eye</u>, <u>ai</u>sle, g<u>ui</u>de, b<u>uy</u>

Word ending spelling patterns

- When adding 'ing' to words with a final silent 'e' (as with '**smile**', '**hide**'), it is usual to remove the final 'e' before adding 'ing'. For example: smiling; hiding;

- When adding 'es' or 'ed' to words with a final 'y', (such as 'supply', 'reply', 'cry'), it is usual to change the 'y' to 'i' before adding 'es' or 'ed'. For example:

supply	supplies	supplied
reply	replies	replied
cry	cries	cried

However, in words such as 'buy' (where 'y' follows a vowel) just add 's' as in '**buys**'.

Spelling Practice

Complete the crossword below.
All the words contain the same vowel <u>sound</u> as in '**like**' but are written with the letters
'i', 'igh', 'y' or 'i' + final silent 'e'

Across Clues

1) a happy expression on the face

3) land with water on all sides

5) the amount of money you pay for something

7) the opposite meaning to 'wrong'

9) suggestions about what someone should do

11) bright light in the sky during a storm

13) to study/check again

15) used to express possibility

17) where we see birds, clouds and planes

19) to discover something you had lost

Down Clues

2) a person who flies a plane

4) something you did not expect

6) not confident when meeting people

8) to get to a place after travelling

10) putting words on to paper
   (you are doing this in this exercise)

12) very pleased about something

14) to be similar

16) you use these to see

18) the measurement of hours and days

20) water that has become frozen, solid

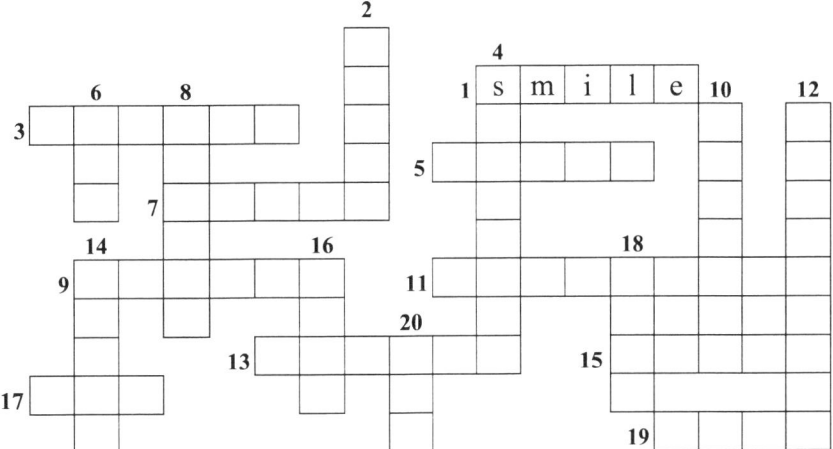

Check your answers on page 74.
Add any incorrectly written words into your spelling reference list (page 91) - making sure
you spell the words correctly in your spelling list for future reference.

Write some rhyming sentences using the words from the spelling lists and crossword.

_____

_____

Read your sentences aloud to revise the pronunciation and spelling.

Vowel sound in the words 'o̲ld', 'bl̲o̲w', 's̲o̲ap'

Check the words 'o̲ld', 'bl̲o̲w', 's̲o̲ap' in your dictionary.

What symbol does your dictionary use to represent the underlined sound in the words?
The symbol in the International Phonetic Alphabet for the vowel s̲o̲und in 'bl̲o̲w' is /əʊ/ in British English and /oʊ/ in North American English.

Read the following sentence aloud. Underline the nine words with the same vowel sound.

Joan wrote a note that told of snow on most of the road that followed the coast.

Check your answers on page 75.

Look at the different ways of s̲pelling this vowel sound.
Add one word from the sentence above to the spelling pattern lists below

Spelling Lists - Ways of spelling the long vowel sound in the word 'road'

o	o + final silent 'e'	ow	oa
o̲nly	h̲o̲pe	kn̲o̲w	soap
w̲o̲n't	ph̲o̲ne	sh̲o̲w	coat

Less usual spelling: t̲o̲e, s̲e̲w, sh̲o̲ulder

Spelling Practice

Complete the crossword below.
All the words contain the same vowel sound but are spelled with 'o' or 'ow'.

Across Clues

1) past tense of 'write'

3) used for smelling and breathing

5) past tense of 'drive'

7) the month before December

9) people ski on this

11) used to speak over long distances

13) opposite to high

15) nearly all (of something)

17) the complete amount

19) to get bigger

21) opposite of 'hot'

Down Clues

2) a fragrant flower

4) opposite of 'yes'

6) opposite to 'under'

8) not working; in need of repair

10) used to travel on water

12) something extra

14) opposite to 'fast'

16) usually made of glass

18) where you live

20) past tense of 'sell'

Check your answers on page 75.

Add any incorrectly written words into your spelling reference list (page 92) - making sure you spell the words correctly in your spelling list for future reference.

Make some rhyming sentences using the words from the previous page and the crossword.

_____

_____

Read your sentences aloud to revise the pronunciation and spelling.

Further Practice

If you are working in a class with other students, you can take turns dictating your sentences for other students to write. This will check your pronunciation and spelling!

Remember!
Your dictionary will show which syllable to stress, in words of more than one syllable (see page 5).

Vowel sound in the words 'n<u>ow</u>', and 'h<u>ou</u>se'

Check the words 'n<u>ow</u>' and 'h<u>ou</u>se' in your dictionary.

What symbol does your dictionary use to represent the underlined sound in the words?
The symbol in the International Phonetic Alphabet for the vowel <u>sound</u> in 'h<u>ou</u>se' is /aʊ/

Read the following sentence aloud. Underline the eight words with the same vowel sound.

Now we can count a thousand brown cows on the mountains to the south of the town.

Check your answers on page 75.

Look at the different ways of <u>spelling</u> this vowel sound.
Add one word from the sentence above to the spelling pattern lists below

Spelling Lists - Ways of spelling the vowel sound in the word 'house'

ow	ou
p<u>ow</u>er	gr<u>ou</u>nd

Spelling Practice

Complete the crossword below.
All the words contain the same vowel sound but are spelled with 'ou' or 'ow'.

Across Clues

1) meaning 'noisy'

3) past tense of the verb 'find'

5) something you can hear

7) the expression on your face when you worry

9) people like to climb or ski down these

11) the letters 'a', 'e', 'i', 'o', 'u'

13) to say something loudly

Down Clues

2) to be unsure, uncertain

4) to permit something

6) a water spray made for decoration

8) sixty minutes

10) this is used to dry things

12) the opposite direction to 'north

14) to say numbers in the correct order

Check your answers on page 75

Add any incorrectly written words into your reference spelling lists (page 92) - making sure you spell the words correctly in your spelling list for future reference.

Make some rhyming sentences using the words from the previous page and the crossword.

Read your sentences aloud to revise the pronunciation and spelling.

Further Practice

If you are working in a class with other students, you can take turns dictating your sentences for other students to write. This will check your pronunciation and spelling!

Remember!
Your dictionary will show which syllable to stress, in words of more than one syllable (see page 5).

General information about English vowel sounds and spelling

Remember!

- Each English vowel letter can be pronounced as a short sound **and** one or more long sounds.

- Your dictionary can help you to understand how words are pronounced.

- Many written English words follow spelling patterns that you can learn.

Useful spelling patterns to remember
Short vowel sounds

A single vowel letter is generally pronounced as a **short sound** when it is followed by a single consonant letter in short words, as in the following examples:

<u>ta</u>p   k<u>i</u>t   n<u>o</u>t   h<u>a</u>t   <u>u</u>s

Long vowel sounds

When you add the letter 'e' onto the end of a word with a short vowel, generally the short vowel sound changes to a longer vowel sound. Look at the following examples:

Add letter 'e' to the end of short words with a short 'a' and it changes the 'a' sound to a longer sound.	Add letter 'e' to the end of short words with a short 'i' and it changes the 'i' sound to a longer sound.
tap (short vowel) tape (longer vowel sound) hat ⟶ hate mat mate	kit (short vowel) kite (longer vowel sound) bit ⟶ bite quit quite

Add letter 'e' to the end of short words with a short 'o' and it changes the 'o' sound to a long sound.	Add letter 'e' to the end of short words with a short 'u' and it changes the 'u' sound to a long sound.
not (short vowel) note (longer vowel sound) cod ⟶ code hop hope	us (short vowel) use (longer vowel sound) cut ⟶ cute tub tube

Note: There are several exceptions to the above pattern. For example, the vowel sound in the words 'give' /gɪv/ and 'have' /hæv/, though ending in 'e', are pronounced with a short vowel sound. Always check your dictionary if you are unsure.

More general spelling rules:

For the following words, pronounced with the long vowel sound /i:/, a general spelling rule is:

Put 'i' before 'e', except after 'c'.

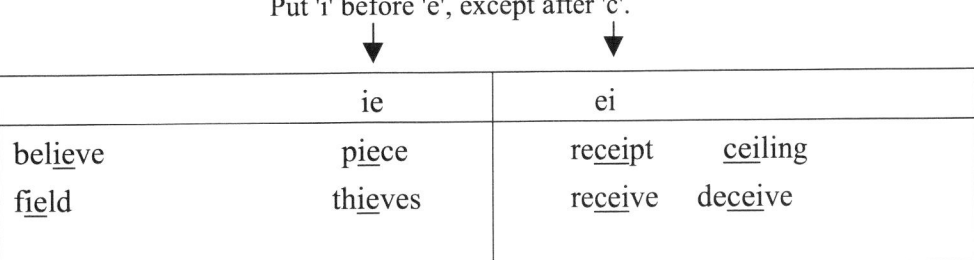

	ie	ei	
beli<u>e</u>ve	p<u>ie</u>ce	rec<u>ei</u>pt	<u>ce</u>iling
f<u>ie</u>ld	thi<u>e</u>ves	re<u>ce</u>ive	de<u>ce</u>ive

Adding 'ing' or 'ed'

- When adding 'ing' **to words with a final silent 'e'** (as with 'smi**le**', 'hi**de**'), it is usual to remove the final 'e' before adding 'ing'.

For example: smile   smiling

hide   hiding

rate   (remove the final 'e' before adding 'ing')   rating

vote   voting

please   pleasing

Adding 'es', 'er' or 'ed'

- When adding 'es', 'er' or 'ed' **to verbs with a final 'y'**, (such as 'supply', 'reply', 'cry'), it is usual to change the 'y' to 'i' before adding 'ed' or 'es'.

For example:

supply   suppl**ied**   suppl**ies**   suppl**ier**

reply   (change the 'y' to 'i')   repl**ied**   repl**ies**   repl**ier**

cry   cr**ied**   cr**ies**   cr**ier**

Note: No change is necessary when adding 'ing' to these verbs eg. supplying, replying, crying.
      No change is necessary in words ending in 'y', if 'y' is preceded by a vowel eg. st<u>a</u>yed, b<u>u</u>ying.

Irregular spelling changes you will have to memorise
Plural nouns

Many English nouns become plural nouns by changing vowel letters (and pronunciation).
Some examples are:

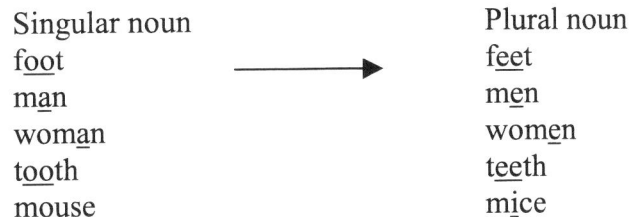

Singular noun		Plural noun
f<u>oo</u>t	→	f<u>ee</u>t
m<u>a</u>n		m<u>e</u>n
wom<u>a</u>n		wom<u>e</u>n
t<u>oo</u>th		t<u>ee</u>th
m<u>ou</u>se		m<u>i</u>ce

Irregular spelling changes you will have to memorise

Past tense verbs

Many English verbs become past tense verbs by the changing of vowel letters (and pronunciation).

Some examples are:

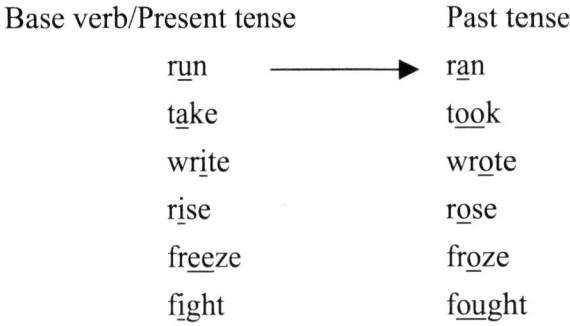

Base verb/Present tense	Past tense
run	ran
take	took
write	wrote
rise	rose
freeze	froze
fight	fought

For a more complete list of these verbs (which are called **irregular** past tense verbs) see page 96.

Note: In some cases, when a verb becomes past tense, the **consonant letters also change**.
Some examples are:

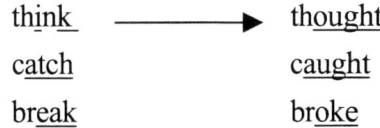

think	thought
catch	caught
break	broke

You can learn more about the pronunciation of English in a book and audio material:

'Understanding English Pronunciation – an integrated practice course'

See final page for details.

Part Three - Spelling patterns

The Consonant letters and sounds of English

In this section you will:

- see and hear the spelling and pronunciation patterns of English consonants

- see the different ways of spelling English consonant sounds

- use your dictionary to learn and understand the pronunciation of new words

- learn some 'rules' you can apply to your spelling

- write the spelling in a 'crossword activity' to reinforce correct spelling

- write some sentences using rhyming words to revise spelling

- read your rhyming sentences to revise your pronunciation.

General Information about English consonant letters and sounds

English consonant letters include **b c d f g h j k l m n p q r s t v w x y z.**

- The consonant letters (**b, d, f, j, k, l, m, n, p, r, t, v, w, z**) each **represent one sound** only, but some of these can also be 'silent' letters. For example, the letter 'w' is not pronounced in the word 'write'; the letter 'b' is not pronounced in the word 'climb'. In these words, 'w' and 'b' are **silent letters**. The letter 'g' is silent in sign, design, length.

  You will have more practice with silent consonant letters on pages 41- 43.

- Some consonant **letters are used together to represent one sound**. For example:

  The letters '**th**' together represent the first sound in **th**ing.

  The letters '**sh**' together represent the first sound in **sh**e.

  The letters '**ph**' together represent the first sound in **ph**one.

  The letters '**ch**' together represent the first sound in **ch**eck.
  (Note: the letters '**tch**' represent the same sound at the end of words, as in ca**tch**, ma**tch**)

  The letters '**dg**' together with a final 'e' represent the last sound in e**dge**, fri**dge**, bri**dge**.

  The letter '**q**' is almost always followed by the letter '**u**'. For example: **qu**ick, **qu**iet, **qu**ote.

- Some consonant letters **represent more than one sound**. For example:

  The letter '**c**' can be pronounced as the sound /k/ in **c**at and the sound /s/ in **c**ent.

  The letter '**s**' can be pronounced as the sound /s/ in **s**it and the sound /z/ in hi**s**.

  The letter '**g**' can be pronounced as the sound /g/ in **g**et and the sound /dʒ/ in pa**g**e.

- Many English words contain a group of consonant sounds following each other, as in the word, **strength**. These groups of consonants, 'str' and 'ngth', in the word 'strength', are called **consonant clusters**. You will have more practice with consonant clusters on pages 54 - 58.

Silent consonants

In English, many written words contain consonant letters that are not pronounced.
These letters are referred to as 'silent' letters.

- Read aloud the words in the box below or ask a fluent speaker of English to read the words.

- Draw a line through the 'silent' letter in each word.

- Match each word with the appropriate meaning below.

- Check the words in your dictionary if you are unsure of the pronunciation or meaning.

rhyme	often	listen	island	calm	column
talk	foreign	hour	exhausted		

- frequently   often*

- sixty minutes   _____

- land surrounded by water   _____

- peaceful and quiet   _____

- words containing the same sounds   _____

- to hear and give attention when someone speaks   _____

- to speak   _____

- to be very tired and without energy   _____

- from another country or another place   _____

- a strong, tall piece of stone or wood used to support a building   _____

*Note: the word 'often' is generally pronounced with a silent 't', though some speakers do pronounce the sound 't' in this word.

Check your answers on page 75.

More silent consonants

A)

- Read aloud the words in the box below or ask a fluent speaker of English to read the words.

- Draw a line through the 'silent' letter in each word.

- Match each word with the appropriate meaning below.

- Check the words in your dictionary if you are unsure of the pronunciation or meaning.

plumber	doubt	debts	wrap
knock	limbs	wrists	knife

- to cover completely with paper or other material _____ *wrap* _____

- a person who repairs water pipes _____

- to be uncertain _____

- where your hands join your arms _____

- to hit or strike something on another thing _____

- money owed to other people _____

- a sharp tool used for cutting _____

- arms, legs or branches of trees _____

  Check your answers on page 76.

B)

Draw a line through the 'silent' letter in each word below then do the exercise on the next page.

climb	know	wrong	knee	lamb
comb	knot	wrote	knew	doubted
knocked	answer	write	sign	walk

There are some patterns with the use of silent consonants.

Can you see which letters can go together?

Silent consonants

C) Complete the information about silent consonants and write some examples.

Write more examples of each pattern on the lines below.

Silent 'b' can follow   *m*   *lamb*   _____   _____

At the beginning of words,
silent 'k' can go before   _____   _____   _____   _____

At the beginning of words,
silent 'w' can go before   _____   _____   _____   _____

You can check your answers on page 76.

Practice with silent consonants

D) Complete the following story with an appropriate word from one of the boxes on the previous page. Note: Not all words in the boxes are used in the story and <u>some words can be used more than once.</u>

The Unlucky Plumber

As the _____ examined a blocked water pipe, he _____ he would

have to _____ over the high fence to remove some large _____ from the

old tree before he could find the cause of the problem. But as he was climbing,

he _____ his leg against the sharp edge of his _____ and cut his _____.

He got such a shock when he saw the deep cut that he fell to the ground and broke

both his _____ as a result of the fall.

An hour later, as he sat in the hospital watching the doctor _____ a bandage

around his badly cut _____ , he asked how long it would be before he

would be able to go back to work. The doctor's _____ was that the cut on

the _____ was not the main problem – he would be able to _____ on his

leg within a few days. However, the doctor suggested it would be many weeks

before he'd be able to _____ with both his _____ set in plaster. The plumber

sighed. He _____ that he'd be able to pay his many _____ that month.

Check your answers on page 76. Add any incorrectly written words into your spelling reference list (page 93) - making sure you spell the words correctly in your spelling list for your future reference.

Consonant <u>sound</u> /f/ in 'f̲our', 'lau̲g̲h', 'p̲h̲one'

There are three ways of spelling the sound /f/.
Notice that in the words **lau̲g̲h** and **p̲h̲one**, the letter combinations 'ph' and 'gh' are pronounced as the sound /f/.

Read the following sentence aloud. Underline the seven words that contain the consonant sound /f/.

I laughed when I found a funny pamphlet about fixing an elephant's cough.

Check your answer on page 77.

Look at the different ways of <u>spelling</u> this consonant sound.
Add one word from the sentence above to the spelling pattern lists below.

Spelling Lists - Ways of spelling the consonant sound in the word 'f̲ull'.

f	ph	gh
f̲ather	telep̲h̲one	enou̲g̲h
f̲ill	grap̲h	

Spelling Practice

Complete the crossword below.
All the words contain the same consonant sound /f/ but are written with 'f', 'ph' or 'gh'.

Across Clues

1) a group of words that express an idea

3) people walk on these

5) the people who are related to you

7) move behind someone; go the same way

9) you use a camera to make one of these

11) to make someone do something

13) you do this when something is funny

15) used to cool air by moving it around

17) a very large animal with a long nose

Down Clues

2) relating to the body

4) used to speak over long distances

6) not many

8) a very thin booklet containing information

10) something to keep animals inside a field

12) not smooth

14) not too much and not too little but…

16) not costing any money

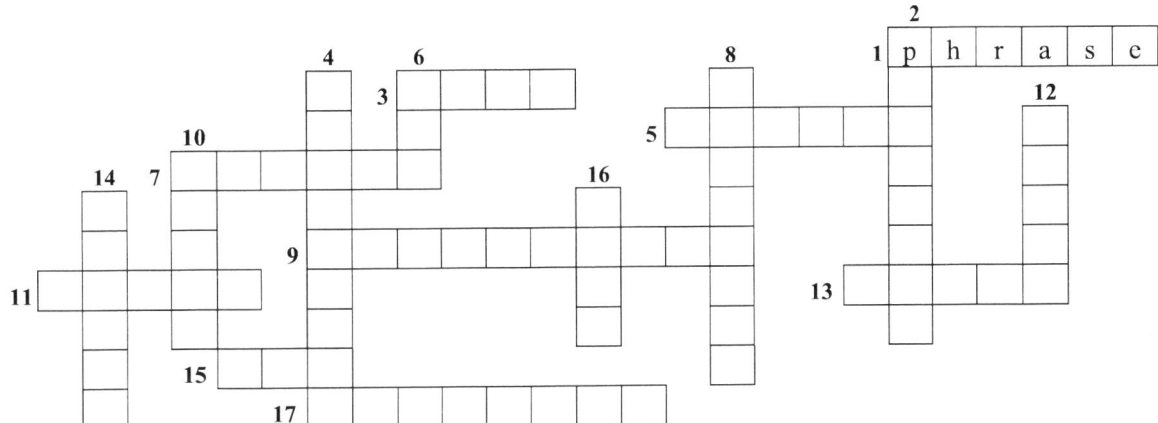

Check your answers on page 77.

Add any incorrectly written words into your spelling reference list (page 93) - making sure you spell the words correctly in your spelling list for your future reference.

Make some rhyming sentences using the words from the previous page and the crossword.

Read your sentences aloud to revise the pronunciation and spelling.

Further Practice

If you are working in a class with other students, you can take turns dictating your sentences for other students to write. This will check your pronunciation and spelling!

Remember!
Your dictionary will show which syllable to stress, in words of more than one syllable (see page 5).

Consonant <u>sound</u> in 'ship', 'sure' 'action'

Check the words, 'ship', 'sure', 'action' in your dictionary.

What symbol does your dictionary use to represent the underlined sound in the words?
The symbol in the International Phonetic Alphabet for the consonant <u>sound</u> in 'ship' is /ʃ/.

Read the following sentence aloud. Underline the eight words with the same consonant sound.

After a short discussion about shops at the station she was sure she had a solution.

Check your answers on page 77.

Look at the different ways of <u>spelling</u> this consonant sound.
Add one word from the sentence above to the spelling pattern lists below

Spelling Lists - Ways of spelling the consonant sound in the word '<u>ship</u>'

sh	s	ss	ti
<u>sh</u>ip	<u>s</u>ugar	pa<u>ss</u>ion	na<u>ti</u>on

Less usual spelling: o<u>ce</u>an, spe<u>ci</u>al, ma<u>ch</u>ine

Spelling Practice

Complete the crossword below.
All the words contain the same consonant sound /ʃ/ but are written with 'sh', 's', 'ss', 'ti',

Across Clues

1) This makes food sweet.

3) This means 'to be certain'.

5) This means 'the way a word is pronounced'.

7) This means 'very good to eat'.

9) the first letter of a name

11) the noun form of 'communicate'

13) to become smaller

15) the noun form of 'express'

17) the noun form of 'discuss'

19) the opposite meaning to 'start'

Down Clues

2) the noun form of 'act'

4) You will find these at the beach.

6) This word means 'not ordinary'.

8) the noun form of 'connect'

10) a country and its people

12) This means 'an important subject or problem'

14) This means 'choice'.

16) The sun does this on a sunny day.

18) These live in the sea.

20) Food is served and eaten from this.

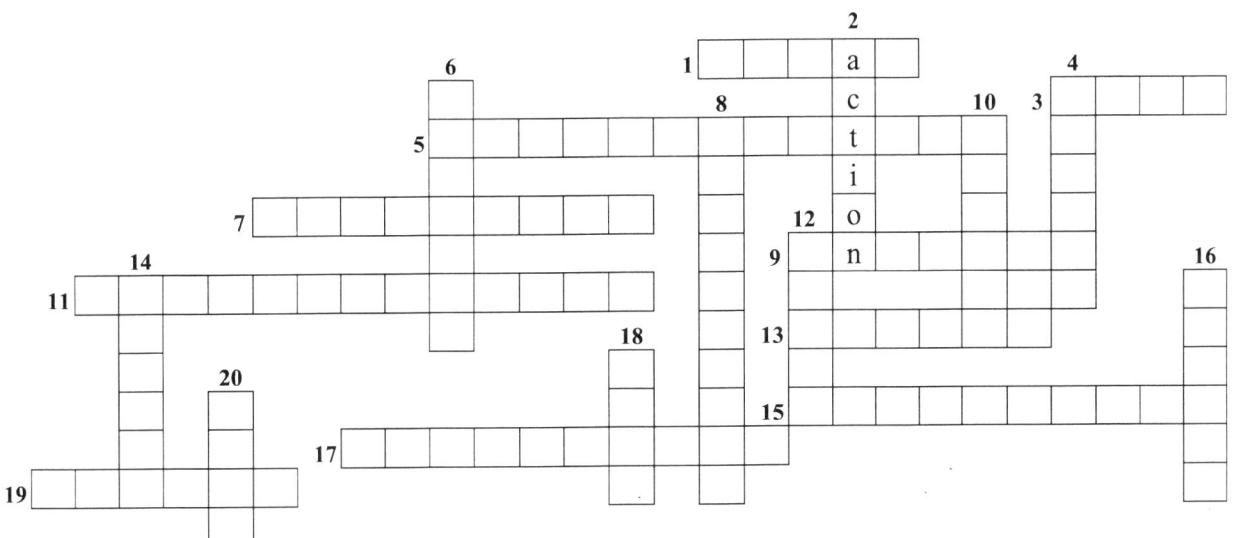

Check your answers on page 77.

Add any incorrectly written words into your spelling reference list (page 94) - making sure you spell the words correctly for future reference.

Make some rhyming sentences using the words from the previous page and the crossword.

_____

_____

Further Practice

If you are working in a class with other students, you can take turns dictating your sentences for other students to write. This will check your pronunciation and spelling!

Remember!
Your dictionary will show which syllable to stress, in words of more than one syllable (see page 5).

Consonant <u>sound</u> in '<u>ch</u>eck', 'fu<u>t</u>ure', 'ma<u>tch</u>'

Check the words, '<u>ch</u>eck', 'fu<u>t</u>ure' 'ma<u>tch</u> in your dictionary.

What symbol does your dictionary use to represent the underlined sound in the words?
The symbol in the International Phonetic Alphabet for the consonant <u>sound</u> in 'ma<u>tch</u>' is /tʃ/.

Read the following sentence aloud. Underline the ten words with the same consonant sound.

**In future I'll check which butcher can deliver cheap chickens
to the kitchen and how much each charges.**

Check your answer on page 77.

Look at the different ways of <u>spelling</u> this consonant sound.
Add words from the sentence above to the spelling pattern lists below

Spelling Lists - Ways of spelling the consonant sound in the word 'ma<u>tch</u>'

ch	tch	t
tea<u>ch</u>	wa<u>tch</u>	na<u>t</u>ure
<u>ch</u>air	ca<u>tch</u>	adven<u>t</u>ure

Less usual spelling: ques<u>ti</u>on

Spelling Practice

Complete the crossword below.
All the words contain the same consonant sound /ʃ/ but are written with 'ch', 'tch', or 't'

Across Clues

1) This is on your face, below your mouth.

3) things such as chairs, tables, beds

5) an exciting experience

7) to examine something to make sure it is correct

9) a word used when asking someone's choice

11) a seat for one person

13) not expensive

15) a room where food is prepared and cooked

17) someone's son or daughter

Down Clues

2) all living things in the world

4) to try to find something by looking carefully

6) the time which is to come (eg. tomorrow)

8) a person who teaches

10) a small stick used for starting fire

12) a drawing or painting of something

14) these are on each side of your nose

16) to look at and give attention to something

18) You do this when someone throws a ball to you.

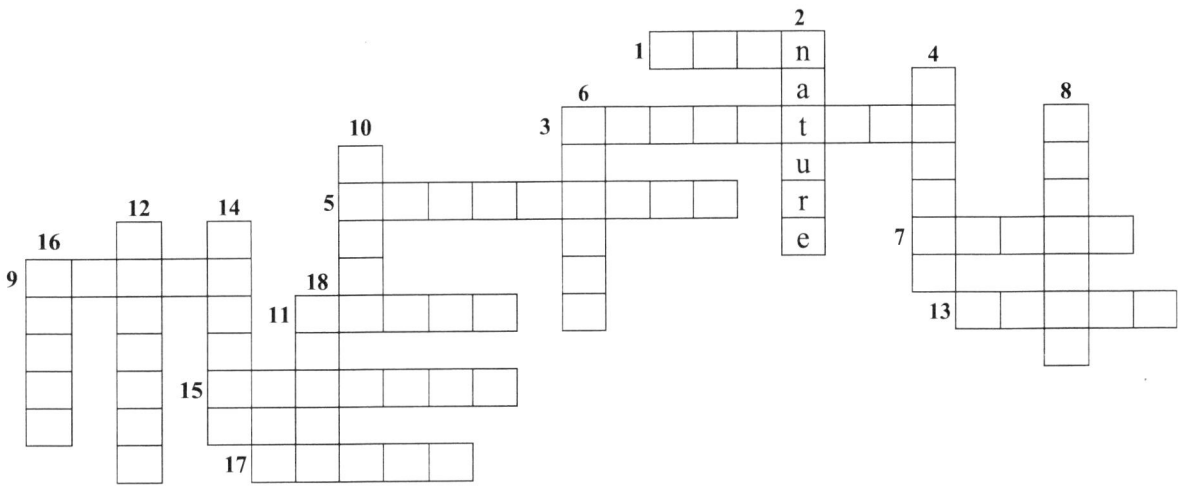

Check your answers on page 77.

Add any incorrectly written words into your spelling reference list (page94) - making sure you spell the words correctly for future reference.

Make some rhyming sentences using the words from the previous page and the crossword.

_____

_____

Further Practice

If you are working in a class with other students, you can take turns dictating your sentences for other students to write. This will check your pronunciation and spelling!

Remember!
Your dictionary will show which syllable to stress, in words of more than one syllable (see page 5).

The consonant letter 'c' can be pronounced two ways:

- 'c' can be pronounced as the sound /k/ as in **cat, collect, act, come**.
  This is the most common way of pronouncing the letter 'c'.

- 'c' can be pronounced as the sound /s/ as in **city**.

The following section provides practice with words written with 'c' but pronounced /s/.

Consonant letter 'c' pronounced as sound /s/ as in cents, circle, peace

Notice in the words **cents, circle, peace** that the letter 'c' is pronounced as the sound /s/.

Read the following sentence aloud. Underline the nine words with the same consonant sound. (Note that in the following sentence, the letter 'c' is pronounced as /s/ in nine of the words; only one letter 'c' is pronounced /k/.

The city celebrated twice in December with an exciting circus, and excellent dancing and racing.

Check your answers on page 78, then read the general spelling/pronunciation guidelines below for the letter 'c'.

The letter 'c' is generally pronounced as /s/ when followed by the letters 'i', 'e' and 'y' and is pronounced as /k/ when followed by any other letter.

Note that often, in words with double 'c', such as a**cc**ident, a**cc**ept, a**cc**ent, the first 'c' is pronounced /k/, the second is pronounced /s/. However, always check a dictionary if in doubt.

Spelling Practice

Complete the crossword below.
All the words contain the consonant <u>sound</u> /s/, but are <u>written with the letter 'c'</u>.

Across Clues

1) a very large town

3) this is taken when sick to make you better

5) more than one mouse

7) past verb form of 'decide'

9) your eyes, nose and mouth are on this

11) more than once

13) a popular food in Asia

15) people do this on special days

17) less than twice

Down Clues

2) the last month of the year (Use a capital letter.)

4) frozen water

6) pleasant, good

8) middle

10) to move your body and feet to music

12) a room where people work

14) definite, sure

16) a piece of bread or cake

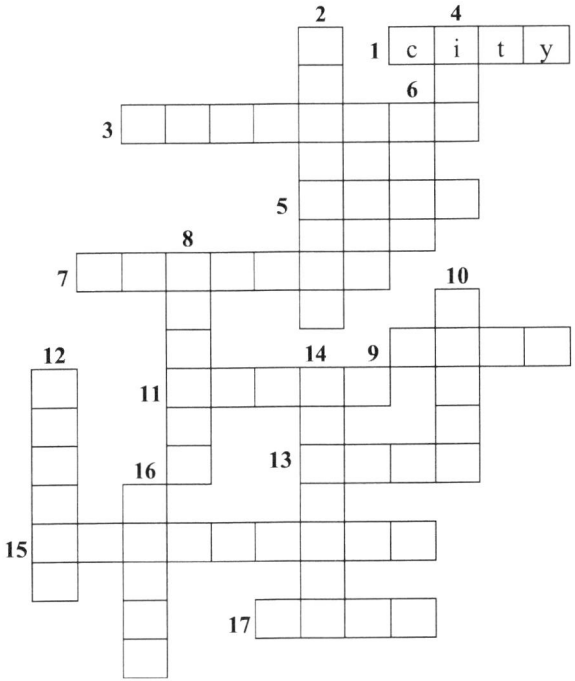

Check your answers on page 78.

Make some sentences using the words from the spelling list and crossword.

_____

_____

Read your sentences aloud to revise the pronunciation and spelling.

Further Practice

If you are working in a class with other students, you can take turns dictating your sentences for other students to write. This will check your pronunciation and spelling!

Remember!
Your dictionary will show which syllable to stress, in words of more than one syllable (see page 5).

The consonant letter 's' can be pronounced two ways:

's' can be pronounced as the sound /s/ as in **s**at, a**s**k, **s**ome.

's' can be pronounced as the sound /z/ as in **is**, **does**, **bu**_s_y.

Note: Many common words such as 'wa_s_', 'hi_s_', 'bu_s_y', are written with the letter 's' but pronounced as the sound /z/.

Read the following sentence aloud. All the words contain the letter 's' but are pronounced with the sound /z/. Underline the sound /z/ in each of the six words.

His busy business is always noisy.

Check you answers on page 78, then do the following exercise.

Read the following clues.
Write the answers in the correct list below, depending on the pronunciation of the letter 's'.

Words pronounced with the sound /s/

1) opposite feeling to happy
2) something you sing
3) a lot of this is found at the beach
4) past verb form of 'sit'
5) one more number than five
6) the one after 'first'
7) you should do this when you see a red traffic light

Words pronounced with the sound /z/

1) this means to say 'no'
2) past verb form of 'is'
3) this means 'belong to him'
4) having a lot of things to do
5) this means 'belonging to her'
6) third person form of 'do'
7) opposite meaning to 'difficult'

Words with the letter 's' pronounced as sound /**s**/	Words with the letter 's' pronounced as sound /**z**/
1) **s**ad	1) refu_s_e /z/

Some guidelines for pronouncing 's':

- The letter 's' is always pronounced /s/ at the beginning of words (except as 'sh')

- The letter 's' is often pronounced /z/ in the middle or at the end of words. If in doubt, check your dictionary.

The consonant letter 'g' can be pronounced two ways:

'g' can be pronounced as the sound /g/ as in **'game', 'go'.**
This is the most common way of pronouncing the letter 'g'.

'g' can be pronounced as the sound /dʒ/ as in **'page', 'large', 'gem'**. Check **large** in your dictionary.
What symbol does your dictionary use to represent the final sound?

Read the following sentence aloud. All the words contain the letter 'g' but are pronounced with
the sound / dʒ/. Underline six words with this consonant sound.

The page about the gym had a general range of stages for gentlemen.

Check you answers on page 78, then do the following exercise.

Read the following clues.
Write the answers in the correct list below, depending on the pronunciation of the letter 'g'.

Words <u>beginning</u> with the sound /g/

1) opposite meaning to 'come'
2) a female child
3) something you give as a present
4) the shape of the world (like a ball)
5) you can see through this
6) the opposite meaning to 'bad'
7) wine is made from these

Words <u>containing</u> the sound /dʒ/ as in 'age'

1) a precious stone
2) meaning 'not detailed or definite'
3) the opposite meaning to 'small'
4) an indoor place for sport and exercise
5) meaning 'unusual'
6) to make something different
7) the number of years a person has lived

Words beginning with the letter 'g' pronounced /**g**/	Words containing letter 'g' pronounced as sound /dʒ/
1) **g**o	1) **g**em

Some guidelines for pronouncing 'g':

- The letter 'g' is always pronounced /g/ before another consonant sound (as in **gl**ass, **gr**een)
  or before the letters 'a', 'o' or 'u'.

- The letter 'g' is sometimes pronounced /dʒ/ before 'e', 'y' or 'i'. If in doubt, check your dictionary.

Consonant clusters in English

Many English words contain a consonant sound followed by a vowel sound, as in the words **no**, **man**.

consonant vowel

no

consonant vowel consonant

man

However, many other English words contain a group of consonant sounds following each other, as in the word, **strict.**

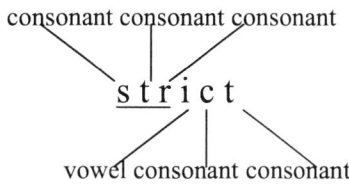

consonant consonant consonant

s t r i c t

vowel consonant consonant

The groups of consonants, 'str' and 'ct', in the word 'strict', are called **consonant clusters**. Words containing consonant clusters may be very challenging for some students of English to pronounce, especially if the consonant sounds are not in their native language.

This section will provide practice in spelling and pronouncing consonant clusters.

Firstly, it is helpful to understand which combinations of letters and sounds are possible in English.

Look at the following consonant letters.

- Draw a line through the letters that are <u>never</u> used together at the <u>beginning</u> of English words.
- Tick ✓ the consonant clusters that <u>are used at the beginning</u> of English words.
- Match the words beginning with a consonant cluster to a picture by writing the complete word. Two have been done as examples. When you have finished, check your answers on page 79.

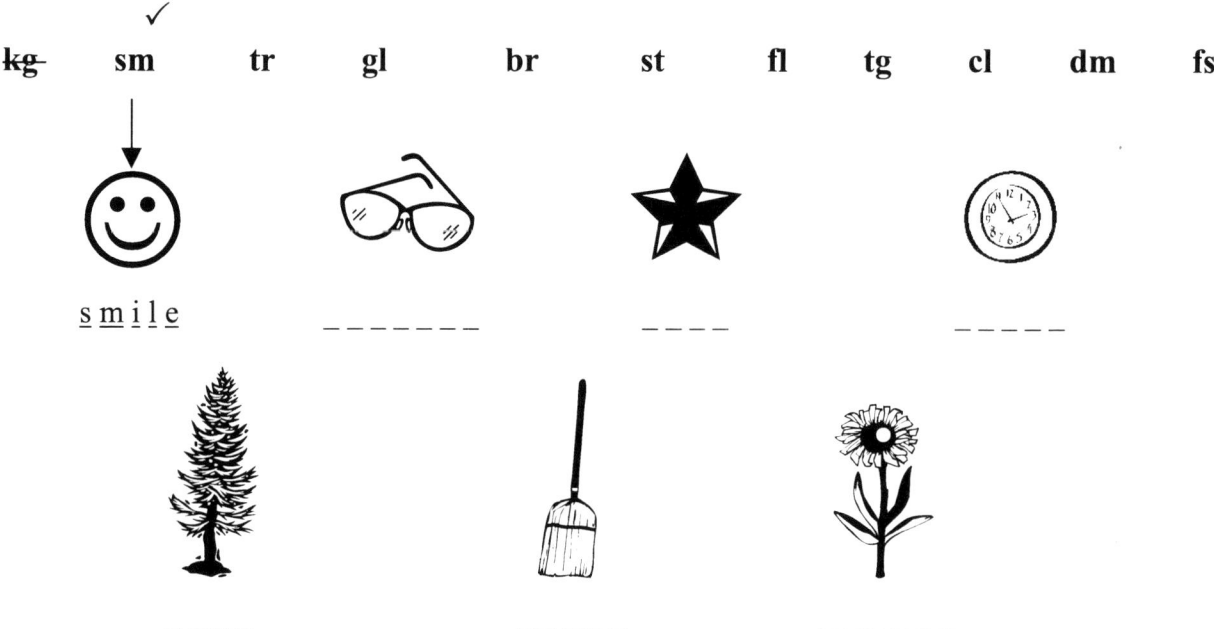

~~kg~~   sm   tr   gl   br   st   fl   tg   cl   dm   fs

s m i l e

_ _ _ _ _ _   _ _ _ _   _ _ _ _ _

_ _ _ _   _ _ _ _ _   _ _ _ _ _ _

In the following section, words with <u>three consonants at the beginning of words</u> will be examined.

Consonant clusters at the beginning of words: str, scr, spr

How many words can you find <u>beginning</u> with the letters **str, scr** or **spr**?
Using a highlighter pen, mark the words appearing Across → and Down ↓ in the box below.
Some words will cross another word.

There are 24 words altogether.

Use your dictionary to help you by finding words beginning with 'scr', 'spr' and 'str' in the dictionary and then checking which words are also in the puzzle below.

When you have found the words, write them in the appropriate lists.
Three have been done as examples.

w	v	s	t	r	a	i	g	h	t	w	s	c	r	e	a	m	b
y	n	b	s	c	r	o	l	l	y	s	c	r	a	t	c	h	o
x	p	s	t	r	e	a	m	z	s	c	r	a	p	e	h	v	l
z	s	t	r	i	n	g	k	w	x	r	e	m	s	n	g	s	s
s	t	r	e	t	c	h	r	p	t	e	w	s	t	r	i	c	t
p	r	a	s	t	r	u	g	g	l	e	q	t	r	v	y	r	r
r	i	y	s	g	w	m	k	l	p	n	w	z	i	t	f	u	e
a	p	s	t	r	o	k	e	h	s	b	r	x	k	l	m	b	e
y	x	w	s	t	r	o	l	l	v	s	p	r	e	a	d	w	t
s	p	r	i	n	k	l	e	x	s	p	r	i	n	g	v	g	x

str

straight   _____

_____   _____

_____   _____

_____   _____

_____   _____

_____

scr

scrub   _____

_____

_____

_____

_____

_____

spr

sprinkle

_____

_____

_____

You can check your answers on page 79.

Consonant clusters at the end of words

How many words can you find in the following puzzle <u>ending</u> with the letters '**ld**'?

Using a highlighter pen, mark the words ending 'ld'. Words appear Across ➔ and Down ↓

There are ten words altogether.
When you have found the ten words, write each one next to the appropriate clue below.

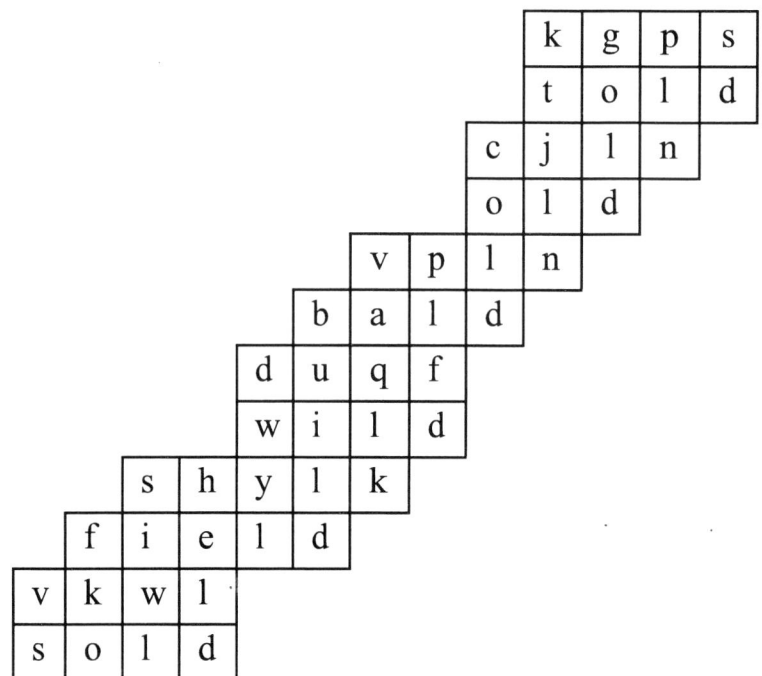

1) This means the opposite to 'young'. _____

2) This describes someone without hair. _____

3) This word means 'to construct' something. _____

4) Past verb form of 'sell'. _____

5) Past verb form of 'hold'. _____

6) A place where sheep or cows eat grass. _____

7) This means the opposite to 'hot'. _____

8) Past verb form of 'tell'. _____

9) This word means 'in its natural state/not controlled'. _____

10) This is a very valuable metal. _____

You can check your answers on page 80.
Read your answers aloud to revise the pronunciation of words ending in 'ld'.

Consonant clusters at the end of words

How many words can you find in the following puzzle <u>ending</u> with the letters '**st**'?

Using a highlighter pen, mark the words ending '**st**'. Words appear Across → and Down ↓

There are fourteen words altogether. (Note: two words have a 'silent' final 'e').
When you have found the fourteen words, write each one next to the appropriate clue below.

```
                              b  u  r  s  t
                           i  n  t  e  r  e  s  t
                           g  u  e  s  t
                        c  h  e  s  t
                     w  o  r  s  t
                  p  a  s  t
            h  o  n  e  s  t
         i  n  s  i  s  t
         x  t  a  s  t  e
```

1) better than anything else _____

2) a person who is invited _____

3) a written or spoken examination _____

4) the time before the present time _____

5) the opposite meaning to 'best' _____

6) A balloon will do this if you stick a pin in it. _____

7) the feeling of wanting to learn more about something _____

8) the front of the body below the neck, above the waist _____

9) to say strongly that something is true or must happen _____

10) to try some food to see if you like it (this word has a final silent 'e') _____

11) the amount of money needed to buy something _____

12) This word describes someone who tells the truth. _____

13) an animal or insect that damages plants or food _____

14) to use too much of something or not use it carefully
    (this word has a final silent 'e'). _____

You can check your answers on page 80.
Read your answers aloud to revise the pronunciation of words ending in 'st'.

Consonant clusters at the end of words

How many words can you find in the following puzzle <u>ending</u> with the letters '**nd**' or '**nk**'?

Using a highlighter pen, mark the words ending **nd** and **nk**. Words appear Across → and Down ↓

- There are fifteen different words. One word is listed twice – can you find which one it is?

- Write one word next to each of the clues below.

					t	r	e	n	d
				t	h	i	n	k	
				h	a	n	d		
			s	a	n	d			
		l	i	n	k				
	b	a	n	k					
b	l	a	n	k					
r	e	s	p	o	n	d			
f	r	i	e	n	d				

1) a change or development in what is happening in society   _____

2) You do this with your brain.   _____

3) This has four fingers and a thumb.   _____

4) There is usually a lot of this at the beach.   _____

5) a connection between people, places or things   _____

6) an institution where you can keep or borrow money   _____

7) a piece of paper which contains no writing or drawing   _____

8) to say or do something as an answer to something   _____

9) a person you know well and like   _____

10) the final part of something

11) the thick, outer skin of lemons and oranges   _____

12) to tell someone you are grateful for something they have done   _____

13) to fall below the surface of the water

14) to arrive on the ground after travel by plane

15) a small group of people who play popular music

- You can check your answers on page 81.

- Read your answers aloud to revise the pronunciation of words ending in '**nd**' and '**nk**'.

Part Four

Spelling in context

In this section you will:

- learn about words that have the <u>same sound</u> but a <u>different spelling</u> pattern

- see how <u>different spelling</u> can indicate <u>different meaning</u>

- see how context can affect which spelling should be used

- use your dictionary to learn which word to use in a particular context

- proofread and correct written texts.

1) Homophones are words that sound the same but have a different spelling pattern.

The pairs of words given in the following exercises sometimes cause spelling errors as they contain the same vowel sound but the different spelling indicates a different meaning. Choose the appropriate word (from the choice of two given for each exercise) and complete the sentences below. Use your dictionary if necessary. You can check your answers on page 81.

right/write

1) Please _____ your name in the _____ side of the page.

wait/weight

2) We'll have to _____for the trolley to help us lift such a heavy _____.

weather/whether

3) They're not sure _____ the _____ will improve by tomorrow morning.

road/rode

4) They _____the tired horses along the dusty _____.

serial/cereal

5) I had a late breakfast of cooked _____ and watched the exciting _____ on TV.

recent/resent

6) I _____a copy of the most _____ magazine as they said the previous copy didn't arrive.

principal/principle

7) The _____ of the school said that the most important _____ to remember was that, 'Honesty is the best policy'.

presents/presence

8) The _____ of the police ensured that the stolen _____ were returned to the correct address.

sight/site

9) The building _____ was an ugly _____ for the tourists.

past/passed

10) I am so happy he's finally _____ his driving test. He's done so much study and practice in the _____few months.

2) Homophones are words that sound the same but have a different spelling pattern.

The pairs of words given in the following exercises sometimes cause spelling errors as they contain the same vowel sound but the different spelling indicates a different meaning.

Choose the appropriate word (from the choice of two given for each exercise) and complete the sentences below. Use your dictionary if necessary. You can check your answers on page 82.

berry/bury

1) When planting young _____ plants, make sure you _____ the roots to the correct depth.

aloud/allowed

2) The sign says the audience isn't _____ to sing _____ as they watch the musical concert.

through/threw

3) The children _____ the ball _____ the hole in the fence.

eight/ate

4) We _____ a large meal at _____ o' clock last night.

border/boarder

5) He is a _____ at an excellent school near the northern _____ of the country.

bare/bear

6) I can't _____ to have my head _____ during the heat of summer – I must wear a hat.

reel/real

7) The young boy wants a _____ fishing line and _____ this summer, rather than the fishing net he used last summer.

tied/tide

8) He _____ the little boat to the wooden post so it wouldn't float away with the strong _____.

sure/shore

9) We are _____ we saw a large crocodile on the _____ of the lake.

meat/meet

10) I'll have to _____ you after I've bought the _____ for dinner.

3) Homophones are words that sound the same but have a different spelling pattern.

The pairs of words given in the following exercises sometimes cause spelling errors as they contain the same vowel sound but the different spelling indicates a different meaning.

Choose the appropriate word (from the choice of two given for each exercise) and complete the sentences below. Use your dictionary if necessary. You can check your answers on page 82.

guest/guessed

1) Have you _____ who the special _____ at tonight's concert is going to be?

peace/piece

2) You won't have any _____ until you give him another _____ of the cake.

paw/poor/pour

3) _____ some warm water over the _____ injured dog's _____.

creek/creak

4) We could hear the tree branches _____ as we walked along the side of the _____.

course/coarse

5) They are renewing the _____ surface of the golf _____ car park to make it smoother.

break/brake

6) Did you _____ the glass of your rear _____ lights when you had the car accident?

ceiling/sealing

7) My husband is _____ the cracks in the _____ before he paints it again.

whole/hole

8) He didn't tell me I had been walking around the _____ day with a _____ in my trousers.

knew/new

9) As soon as I saw the _____ dress, I _____ I had to buy it.

plain/plane

10) Fortunately, the _____ made an emergency landing on the flat, dusty _____.

4) Homophones are words that sound the same but have a different spelling pattern.

The pairs of words given in the following exercises sometimes cause spelling errors as they contain the same vowel sound but the different spelling indicates a different meaning.

Choose the appropriate word (from the choice of two given for each exercise) and complete the sentences below. Use your dictionary if necessary. You can check your answers on page 82.

rows/rose

1) The _____, being a very bright flower, looks best when planted in straight _____.

steel/steal

2) The _____ bars were tied together so that nobody could _____ them.

stares/stairs

3) Have you noticed how everyone _____ at her as she walks down the _____.

stationary/stationery

4) The _____ bus blocked the sign above the entrance to the _____ store.

scent/sent

5) I _____ my friend a card and a bottle of sweet smelling _____ to make her feel better.

seen/scene

6) The accident _____ was the most terrible thing I had ever _____.

to/too/two

7) This box is _____ heavy for _____ people _____ carry – we'll need at least three people.

waist/waste

8) I don't like to _____ delicious food but I can't eat another thing – my _____ is getting too big!

blue/blew

9) The hat suddenly _____ off her head in the strong wind and floated across the _____ water.

*wear/were

10) We _____ going to _____ the same clothes to the party but we've changed our minds.

*The words **were** and **wear** are pronounced a little differently but the spelling of these words is often confused.

Spelling in context – Pronouns: pronunciation and spelling

In spoken language, pronouns are often followed by a contraction.

For example, *'he is'* becomes *he's*; *'we are'* becomes *we're*; *'they are'* becomes *they're*.

In spoken English, these particular pronouns are often confused with other words that have a similar pronunciation. For example, look at the <u>underlined</u> words in the following sentence.

'<u>They're</u> travelling here by bus because <u>their</u> car is being repaired.'

If you read this sentence aloud, you will see that **'their'** and **'they're'** are pronounced similarly. However, these words have different meanings:

> **their** shows possession;
> **they're** is a contracted form of **'they are'**.

Look at the following sentences. The **bold** words in each sentence may be confused as they are pronounced similarly.

- The dog has eaten **its** dinner and now **it's** sitting quietly in the corner.
  (**its** shows possession; **it's** = it is)

- **You're** clever because you always finish **your** homework first.
  (**you're** = you are; **your** shows possession)

- We **were** late for class yesterday, but **we're** going to make sure **we're** early in future.
  (**were** is a past plural verb; **we're** = we are - Note: we're is sometimes pronounced /wɪə/).

- **His** mother said **he's** very lazy. (**his** shows possession; **he's** = he is)
  Note: **'his'** is pronounced with a short vowel /hɪz/; **he's** is pronounced with a long vowel sound /hi:z/, however the correct usage of these words is often confused.

Practice

Complete the sentences below by choosing the correct word from the box and writing it in the appropriate space (using a capital letter where necessary). The underlined pronoun in each sentence will give you a clue about which words to use. You can check your answers on page 83.

their	they're	were	we're	he's	his	you're	your	it's	its

1) _____ camera was stolen while <u>he</u> was overseas last week, and _____ still angry about it.

2) _____very happy with the results of <u>our</u> business trip. We visited over ten companies

   while we _____ overseas.

3) _____ much taller than _____ brother but he's older than <u>you</u>, isn't he?

4) We have a new cat and _____ sitting on the mat. _____ name is Kitty and <u>it</u> eats a lot.

5) _____ daughter has just graduated with excellent results, so _____

   very proud and happy. <u>They</u>'ve just been to the graduation ceremony.

Spelling in context – find the spelling mistakes (1)

There are **twelve** spelling mistakes in the following piece of text. The mistakes are all the kind of mistake that would not be highlighted on your computer 'spell-check' because each is an English word that can be found in the dictionary, however, the spelling is **not correct in the context** below.

Your job is to find the **twelve** mistakes and correct them.
Use your dictionary to check words if you are unsure of the correct spelling.

Time and Change

It's rite to say that life has changed. The pace and stile of life today is not the same as it was in our grandparent's day. Science has changed the weigh of life in almost every place on earth at quiet an amazing pace. I'm shore you can think of many changes that have occurred in your lifetime.

We now have machines that reduce work and make moor free time available to relax each day. Science has developed ways to reduce crime and medicines to take away disease and pane. We can now travel grate distances very quickly by plain or train, where people of the past had to allow a lot of time to walk, ride or sale to far away places. We can now communicate almost immediately by e-mail rather than waiting many daze to receive letters by regular male. Yes - it's impossible to deny that the pace and style of life has changed in many ways!

Check your answers on page 83.

Spelling in context – find the spelling mistakes (2)

There are **fourteen** spelling mistakes in the following piece of text.

Some of the mistakes are the kind of mistake that would not be highlighted on your computer 'spell-check' because it is an English word that can be found in the dictionary but the spelling is **not correct in the context** below. The other mistakes in the text are words that are often written incorrectly.

Your job is to find the **fourteen** mistakes and correct them.
Use your dictionary to check words if you are unsure of the correct spelling.

Sport

From the earliest recorded history through to modern times, sporting events have all ways bean popular. Sum of the earliest known sports are still played today, but many of the details about how sport is played have changed. Four example, in the past women wear not aloud to play some types of sport. Also, some types of sport where only played by wealthy people.

In our modern times, sport can be enjoyed by all most everyone in society, weather they are rich or pour. Not everyone actually plays sport; however, many people who can't play, enjoy watching other people compete in diffrent types of sport. Some people prefer indoor games such as table tennis or darts. Some prefer games such as tennis or squash that are played on a caught. Other people enjoy very active sports such as soccer or hockey.

For many people, sport is their mane form of entertainment and relaxation. On the other hand, there are people who are not interested in sport of any type and think that sport is a complete waist of time. What do you think about sport?

Check your answers on page 84.

Spelling in context - find the spelling mistakes (3)

There are **twenty** spelling mistakes in the following piece of text.

Some of the mistakes are the kind of mistake that would not be highlighted on your computer 'spell-check' because it is an English word that can be found in the dictionary but the spelling is **not correct in the context** below. The other mistakes in the text are words that are often written incorrectly.

Your job is to find the **twenty** mistakes and correct them.
Use your dictionary to check words if you are unsure of the correct spelling.

Health and Happiness

Good health is important to every person, yet many people don't take enough care of there health. Doctors agree that to bee healthy, it's important to have a balanced life. For example, they say it's important to have a balance between work and rest and to get reguler exersise.

However, I'm shore you'd agree that in our busy world, it's not always eazy to get and keep balanse in our lives. Due to financial problems, many people work long ours, leaving little time at the end of their busy weak to spend with their family and frends. They eat quickly and don't get enough rest or relaxation and then their health suffers due too to much stress.

Intrestingly, doctors now agree that having balance in hour lives will bring, not only better health, but also a grater chance of sucsess. If we can keep our lives more balanced, we will have moor energy, and reech our goals in a more relaxed way; without feeling the harmfull effects of stress in our lifes.

Check your answers on page 84.

Spelling in context - find the spelling mistakes (4)

There are **twenty** spelling mistakes in the following piece of text.

Some of the mistakes are the kind of mistake that would not be highlighted on your computer 'spell-check' because it is an English word that can be found in the dictionary but the spelling is **not correct in the context** below. The other mistakes in the text are words that are often written incorrectly.

Your job is to find the **twenty** mistakes and correct them.
Use your dictionary to check words if you are unsure of the correct spelling.

The Challenge of Learning a Language

Learning a new language can be a challenge. For example, when we hear people speaking an unfamiliar language, it maybe difficult to hear were one word finishes and another word begins. The speakers sound as if there speaking much to fast and there words sound as if they are all joined together into one very, very long sentence, without one paws.

This problem can be helped buy understanding the difference between written and spoken language. Four example, in *written* English, words can be seen with spaces between them on a page but in *spoken* English, words are ofen linked together and may be difficult to here as separate words. For this reason, when beginning to learn a knew language, it can be useful to reed and listen to a text at the same time. This method helps learners to become familiar with the weigh speakers link words together.

A use full method for learning new words, is to try to guess the meaning of the words as you read threw the text. When you have red the complete text, check your dictionry to sea if you have guest the meaning correctly.

Remember that learning to understand and speak a new language well doesn't usually happen quickly – it takes time, patients, and a lot of practise.

Check your answers on page 85.

Syllables - Revision

- All spoken words are made with *syllables*.
- A syllable is formed by the linking of individual sounds to form **one unit of unbroken sound within a word**.
- A word can contain one or more syllables. For example: <u>a</u> = one syllable; <u>aloud</u> = two syllables.
- Each syllable generally contains one vowel sound but may contain several consonant sounds.

When trying to remember the spelling of a word, it can be useful to say the word slowly and picture the syllables as you say the word. For example: con-son-ant; Eng-lish; re-mem-ber.

However, when English is spoken at normal conversational speed, *not all syllables in words are pronounced as they are written.* English <u>spelling patterns do not always accurately represent how a word should be pronounced</u>. For this reason, it is very helpful to know how your dictionary can help you with the pronunciation of words.

Below are some commonly used English words that contain syllables that are not usually pronounced when spoken within a conversation, at normal conversational speed.

'Silent' syllables

- Read the sentences aloud, making sure the underlined word is spoken at normal speed (or ask a fluent speaker of English to read the sentences).
- Decide which part of the underlined word is <u>not</u> pronounced.
- Put a bracket ( ) around the part that is <u>not pronounced</u>. The first one has been done as an example.
- Check your dictionary if you are unsure. Many dictionaries will show the unpronounced sound in brackets. You can also check the answers on page 85.

1) This is an <u>int(e)resting</u> book.
2) He visits her <u>every</u> day.
3) This book is <u>different</u> to that one.
4) Where does your <u>family</u> live?
5) I've eaten too much <u>chocolate</u>!
6) What kind of <u>business</u> is it?
7) I've seen that movie <u>several</u> times.
8) I just bought a new <u>camera</u>.
9) This is a good <u>reference</u> book.
10) They work at the same place, but in a <u>separate</u> building.
11) This chair is very <u>comfortable</u>.
12) He works in a small <u>factory</u>.
13) What was the <u>temperature</u> today?
14) The <u>average</u> family watches too much television

A final note:

Remember! Many English words can be divided into syllables to help you remember the spelling pattern. However, as you have seen from the exercises in this book, there are some words that contain silent letters, silent syllables or don't fit into a spelling pattern.

For this reason, spelling practice should involve both your **eyes** and your **ears.**

- Learning the spelling and pronunciation of new words should include **reading**, **listening**, **writing** and **speaking** the words so that you see the connection between the written and spoken forms.

- Develop the habit of checking words in your dictionary whenever you are unsure of a word!

   Best wishes in your future learning experiences!

Part 5 – Answers

Introduction to the spelling and pronunciation of English – Revision

1) How many <u>letters</u> are there in written English?   **26**

2) How many <u>sounds</u> are used in spoken English?   **more than 40**

3) What do dictionaries and pronunciation text books
  use to explain the sounds of English letters and words?   **symbols**

Vowel sound in the word 'f<u>u</u>n', 'm<u>o</u>nth', 'c<u>ou</u>sin'

My h<u>u</u>ngry y<u>ou</u>ng br<u>o</u>ther l<u>o</u>ves b<u>u</u>tter and h<u>o</u>ney.

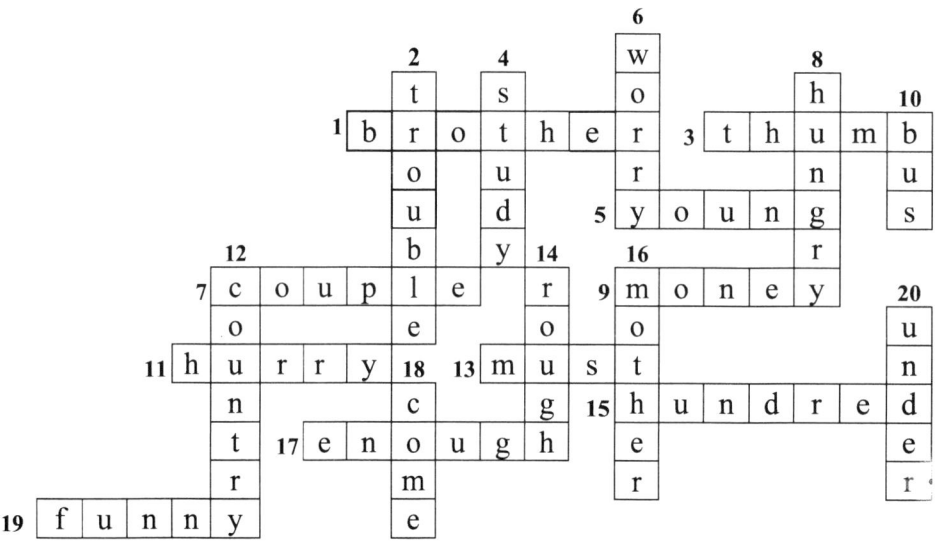

17 Across Note: words with 'gh' as in the word **enough** (pronounced /f/) are practiced in the Consonant section.

Vowel sound in the words 'p<u>i</u>nk', 't<u>y</u>pical', 'b<u>ui</u>lding'

The pr<u>e</u>tty ch<u>i</u>ldren s<u>i</u>t and dr<u>i</u>nk m<u>i</u>lk and the b<u>u</u>sy w<u>o</u>men v<u>i</u>sit the g<u>y</u>m <u>i</u>n the b<u>i</u>g p<u>i</u>nk b<u>ui</u>lding.

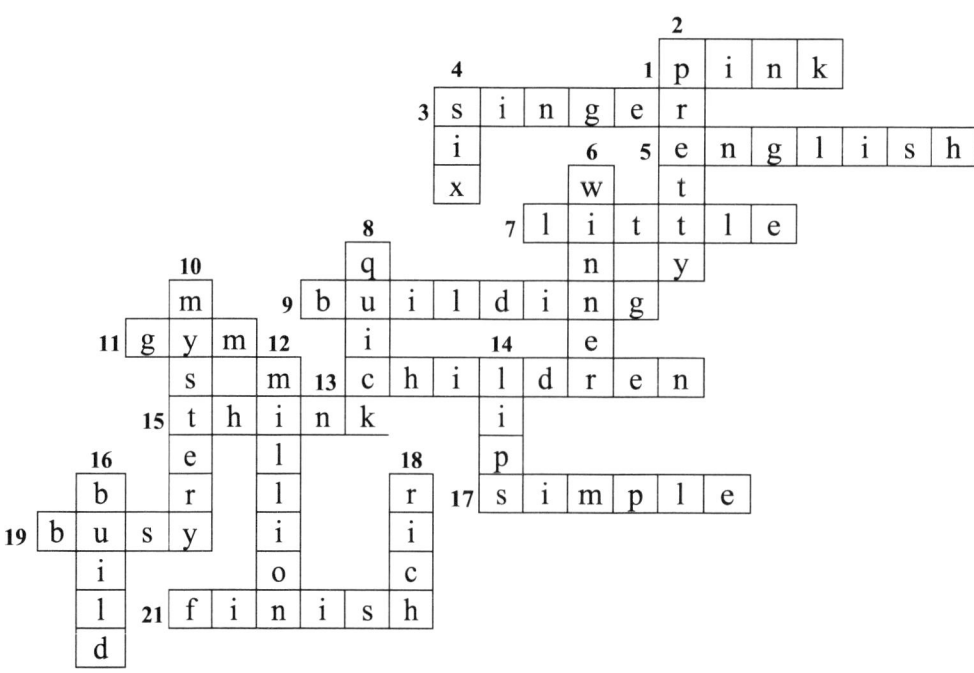

Note: The word <u>E</u>nglish will always begin with a capital letter when written.

Vowel sound in the words 'any', 'red', 'bread'

Ten guests had many suggestions for better health, wealth and less stress.

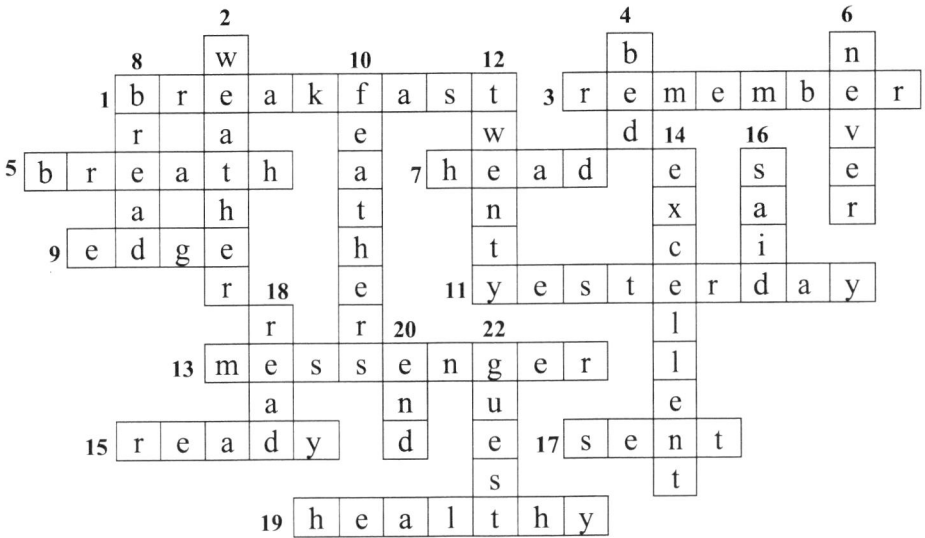

Vowel sound in the words 'what', 'hot', 'stop'

Tom lost his wallet and watch when the shop got robbed.

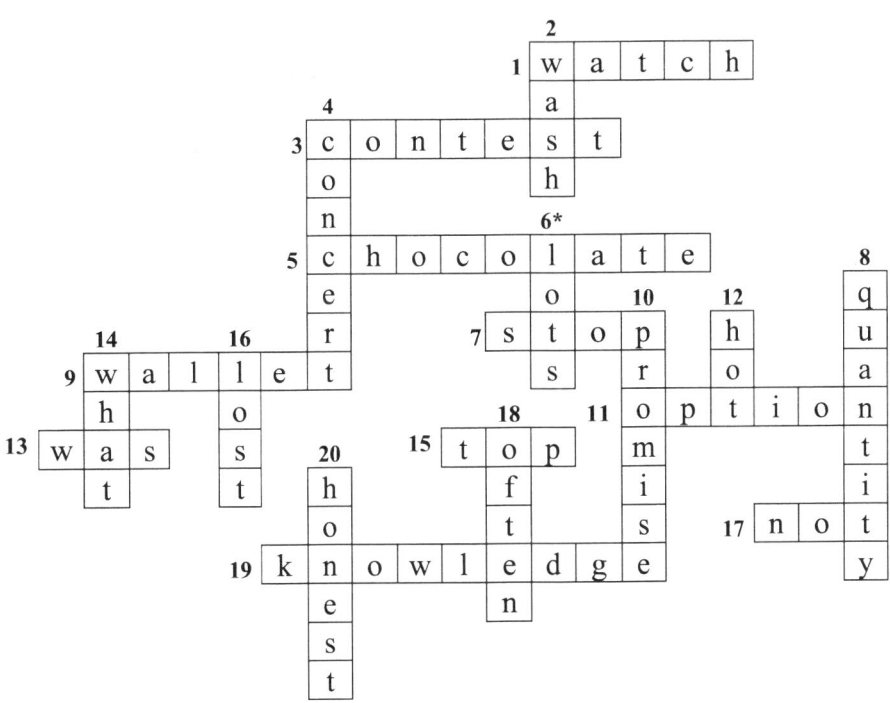

Note on 6*: '<u>lots</u> of something' can also be expressed as '<u>a lot</u> of something'

Vowel sound in the words 'sugar', 'could', 'good'   Answers

The c<u>oo</u>k b<u>oo</u>k says we sh<u>oul</u>d p<u>u</u>t a f<u>ull</u> spoon of s<u>ug</u>ar in the c<u>oo</u>kies.

The word 'spoon' contains the longer vowel sound /u: / and so is pronounced differently to the underlined words.

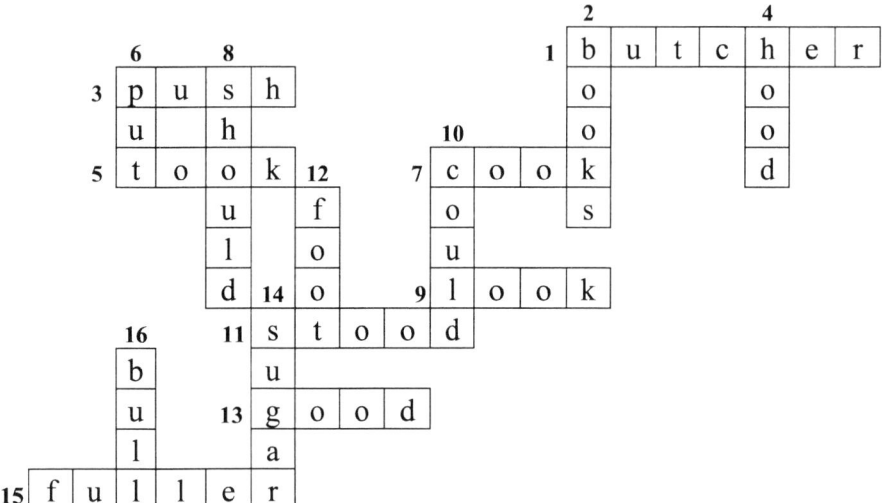

Vowel sound in the word 'green', 'leaves', 'field'

Sh<u>e</u> bel<u>ie</u>ves the r<u>ea</u>son w<u>e</u> <u>ea</u>t gr<u>ee</u>n ch<u>ee</u>se is <u>ea</u>sy to s<u>ee</u> but h<u>e</u> f<u>ee</u>ls sh<u>e</u>'s dec<u>ei</u>ved.

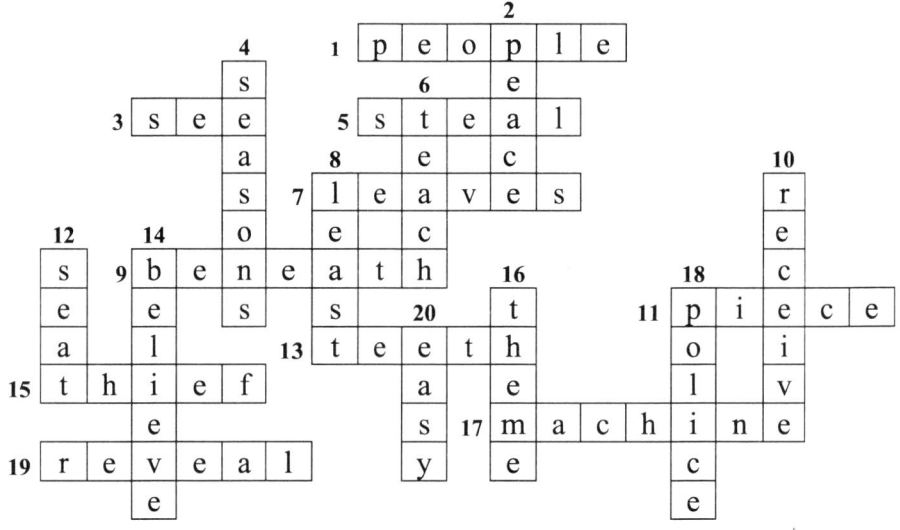

Vowel sound in the word 'move', 'soon', 'rule'

The sch<u>oo</u>l r<u>u</u>les about m<u>o</u>ving comp<u>u</u>ters thr<u>ough</u> r<u>oo</u>ms will s<u>oo</u>n be appr<u>o</u>ved.

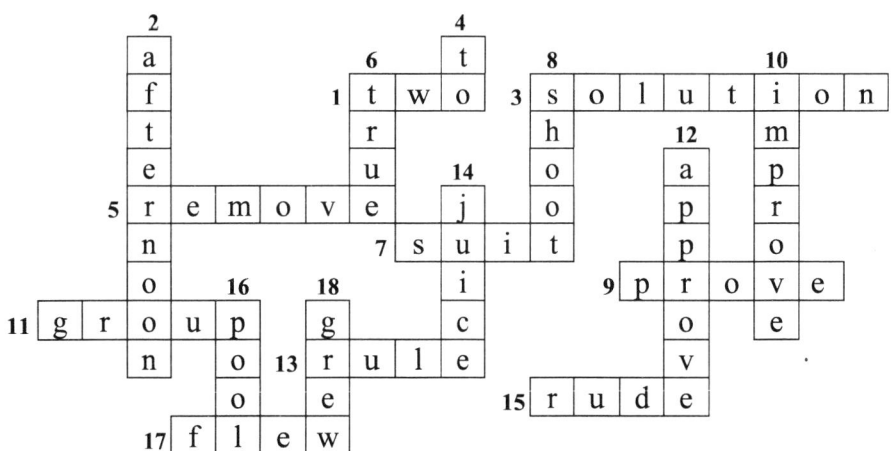

Vowel sounds 'b<u>ir</u>d', 'w<u>or</u>d', 'p<u>ur</u>ple'

Th<u>ir</u>ty g<u>ir</u>ls in p<u>ur</u>ple sk<u>ir</u>ts will ret<u>ur</u>n to w<u>or</u>k <u>ear</u>ly next t<u>er</u>m.

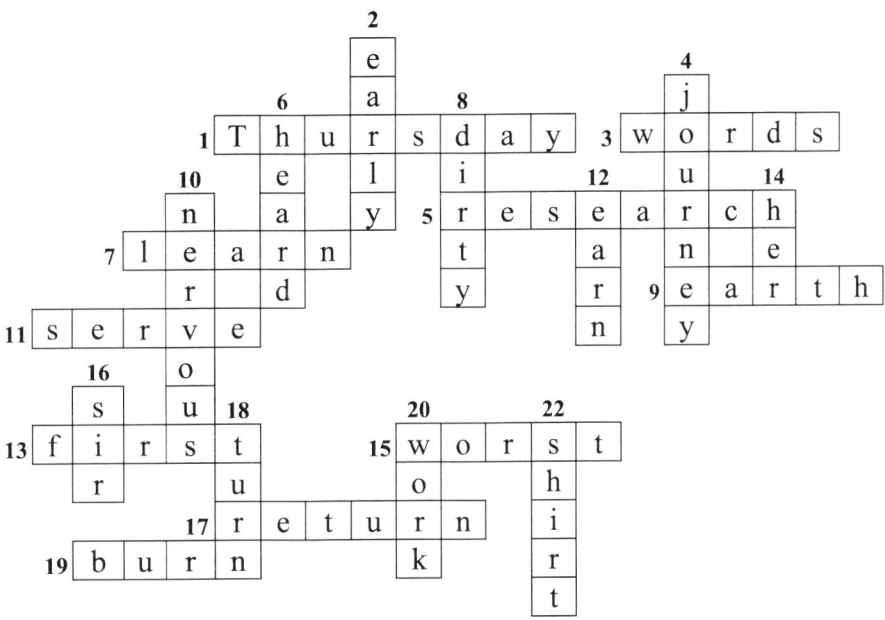

Vowel sound in the words 'f<u>ou</u>r', 'w<u>ar</u>m', 'd<u>oo</u>rs'

This m<u>or</u>ning they w<u>ar</u>ned of f<u>ou</u>r m<u>o</u>re st<u>or</u>ms tow<u>ar</u>ds the sp<u>or</u>ts c<u>our</u>ts.

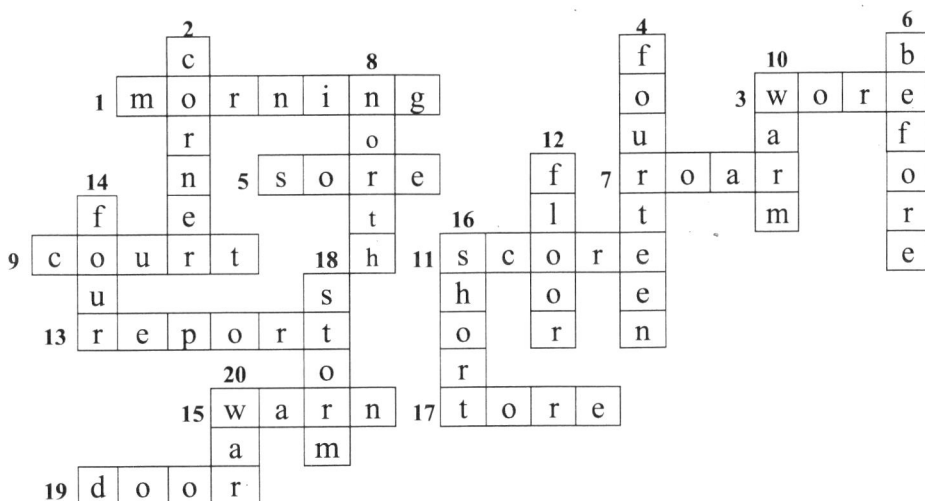

Vowel sound in the words 'v<u>oi</u>ce', 't<u>oy</u>', 's<u>oi</u>l'

The b<u>oy</u>s av<u>oi</u>ded being n<u>oi</u>sy with their t<u>oy</u>s but it sp<u>oi</u>lt their enj<u>oy</u>ment.

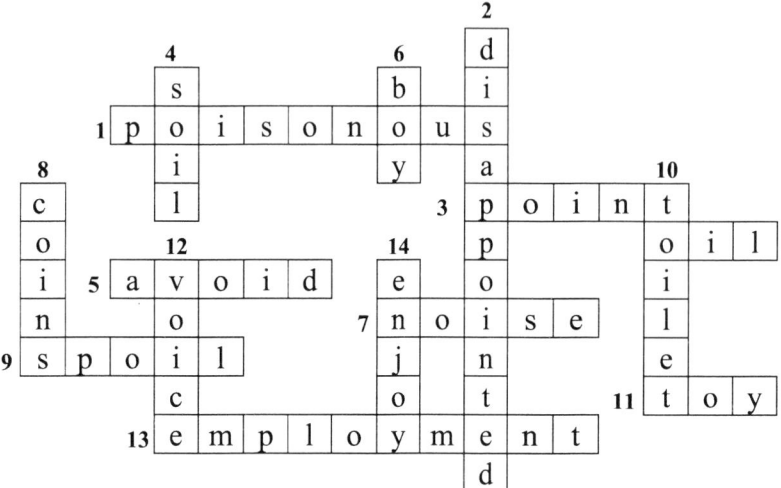

Vowel sound in the words 'd<u>a</u>te', 'w<u>ei</u>ght', 'w<u>ay</u>s'

Th<u>ey</u> st<u>ay</u>ed and w<u>ai</u>ted in the s<u>a</u>me pl<u>a</u>ce as the tr<u>ai</u>n was l<u>a</u>te.

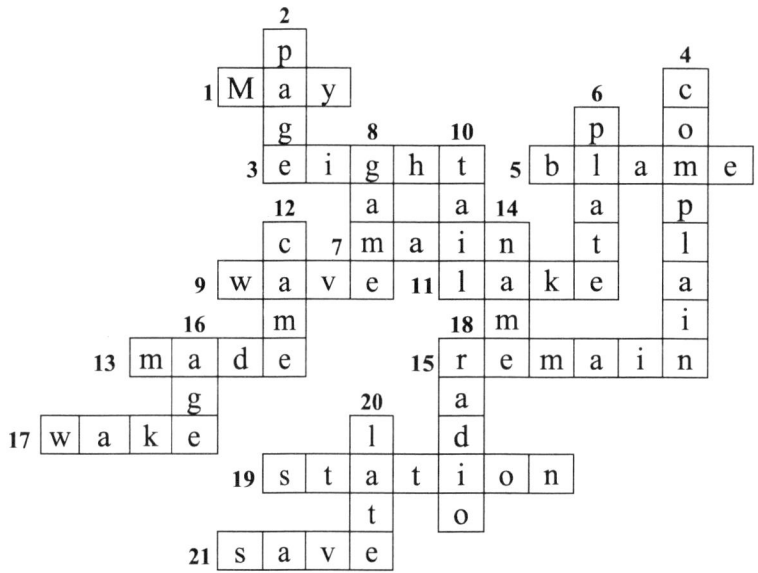

Vowel sound in the words 'wh<u>y</u>', 'br<u>igh</u>t', 'wh<u>i</u>te'

She l<u>i</u>kes k<u>i</u>nd br<u>igh</u>t sm<u>i</u>les, n<u>i</u>ce wh<u>i</u>te w<u>i</u>ne, l<u>i</u>me <u>i</u>ce-cream and fl<u>y</u>ing h<u>igh</u> in the sk<u>y</u>.

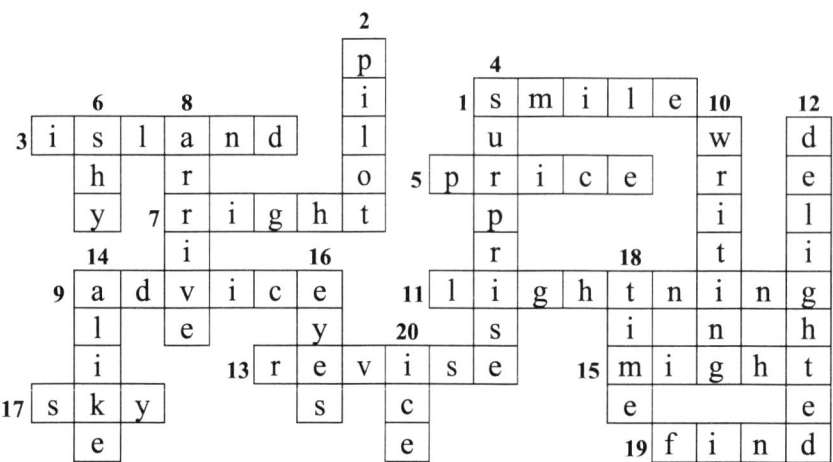

Vowel sound in the words 'old', 'blow', 'soap'

J<u>oa</u>n wr<u>o</u>te a n<u>o</u>te that t<u>o</u>ld of sn<u>ow</u> on m<u>o</u>st of the r<u>oa</u>d that foll<u>ow</u>ed the c<u>oa</u>st.

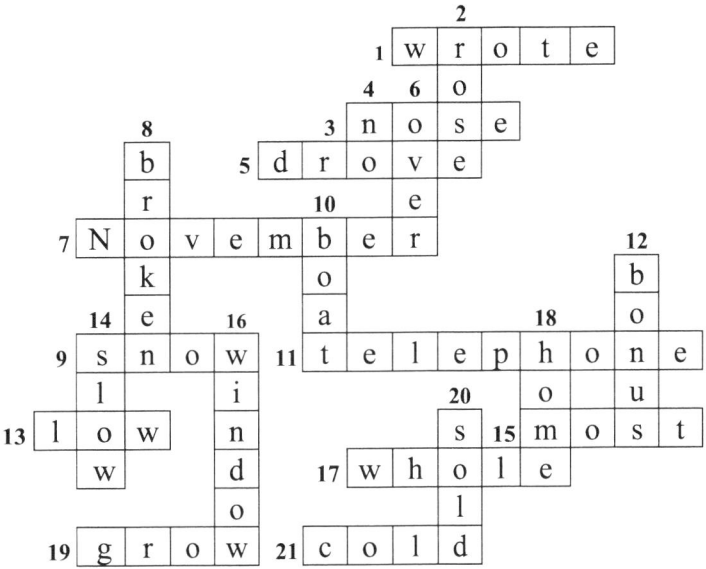

Vowel sound in the words 'now' and 'house'

N<u>ow</u> we can c<u>ou</u>nt a th<u>ou</u>sand br<u>ow</u>n c<u>ow</u>s on the m<u>ou</u>ntains to the s<u>ou</u>th of the t<u>ow</u>n.

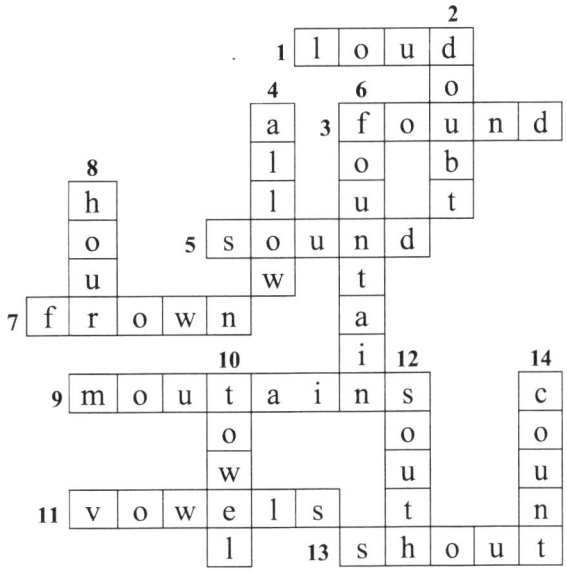

Silent consonants – Answers

- frequently   of~~t~~en*
- sixty minutes   ~~h~~our
- land surrounded by water   is~~l~~and
- peaceful and quiet   ca~~l~~m
- words containing the same sounds   r~~h~~yme
- to hear and give attention when someone speaks   lis~~t~~en
- to speak   ta~~l~~k
- to be very tired and without energy   ex~~h~~austed
- from another country or another place   forei~~g~~n
- a strong, tall piece of stone or wood used to support a building   colum~~n~~

More silent consonants - Answers

A)

- to cover completely with paper or other material _____ *wrap* _____
- a person who repairs water pipes _____ *plumber*
- to be uncertain _____ *doubt*
- where your hands join your arms _____ *wrists*
- to hit or strike something on another thing _____ *knock* _____
- money owed to other people _____ *debts*
- a sharp tool used for cutting _____ *knife*
- arms, legs or branches of trees _____ *limbs*

B)

climb	know	wrong	knee	lamb
comb	knot	wrote	knew	doubted
knocked	answer	write	sign	walk

C)

Silent 'b' can follow _____ *m* _____ *climb* _____ *comb* _____ *lamb*

At the beginning of words,
silent 'k' can go before _____ *n* _____ *knife* _____ *know* _____ *knock*

At the beginning of words,
silent 'w' can go before _____ *r* _____ *write* _____ *wrists* _____ *wrong*

D) The Unlucky Plumber

As the ***plumber*** examined a blocked water pipe, he ***knew*** he would
have to ***climb*** over the high fence to remove some large ***limbs*** from the
old tree before he could find the cause of the problem. But as he was climbing,
he ***knocked*** his leg against the sharp edge of his ***knife*** and cut his ***knee***.
He got such a shock when he saw the deep cut that he fell to the ground and broke
both his ***wrists*** as a result of the fall.

An hour later, as he sat in the hospital watching the doctor ***wrap*** a bandage
around his badly cut ***knee***, he asked how long it would be before he
would be able to go back to work. The doctor's ***answer*** was that the cut on
the ***knee*** was not the main problem – he would be able to ***walk*** on his
leg within a few days. However, the doctor suggested it would be many weeks
before he'd be able to ***write*** with both his ***wrists*** set in plaster. The plumber
sighed. He ***doubted*** that he'd be able to pay his many ***debts*** that month.

Consonant sound /f/ in the words la<u>ugh</u>, <u>f</u>our, <u>ph</u>one   **Answers**

I la<u>ugh</u>ed when I <u>f</u>ound a <u>f</u>unny pam<u>ph</u>let about <u>f</u>ixing an ele<u>ph</u>ant's co<u>ugh</u>.

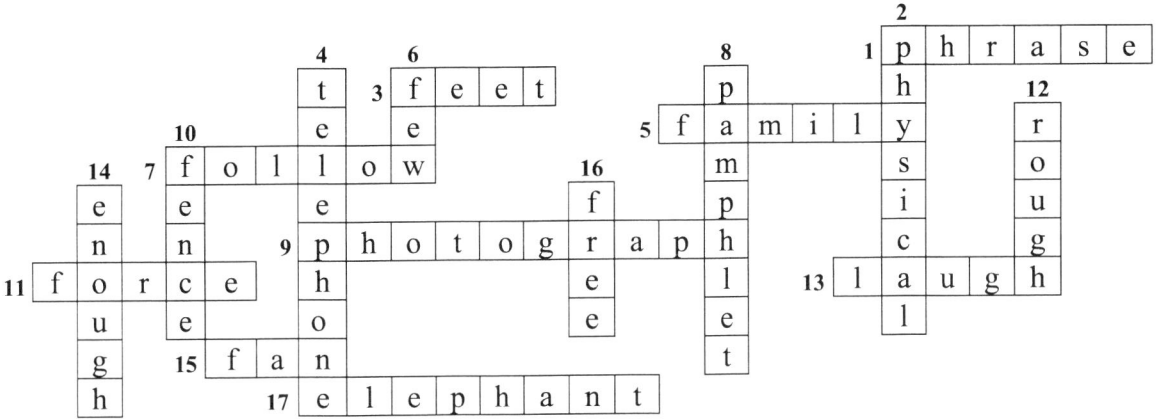

Consonant sound in '<u>sh</u>ip', 'o<u>c</u>ean', 'sta<u>ti</u>on'

After a <u>sh</u>ort discu<u>ss</u>ion about <u>sh</u>ops at the sta<u>ti</u>on <u>sh</u>e was <u>s</u>ure <u>sh</u>e had a solu<u>ti</u>on.

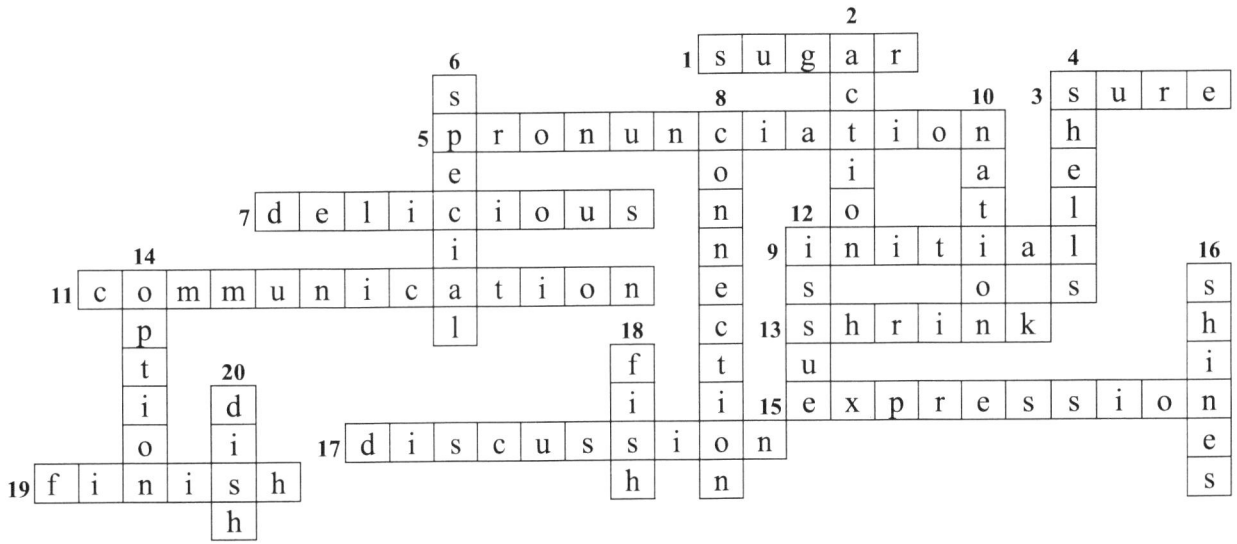

Consonant sound in '<u>ch</u>eck', 'fu<u>t</u>ure', 'ma<u>tch</u>

In fu<u>t</u>ure I'll <u>ch</u>eck whi<u>ch</u> bu<u>tch</u>er can deliver <u>ch</u>eap <u>ch</u>ickens to the ki<u>tch</u>en and how mu<u>ch</u> ea<u>ch</u> <u>ch</u>arges.

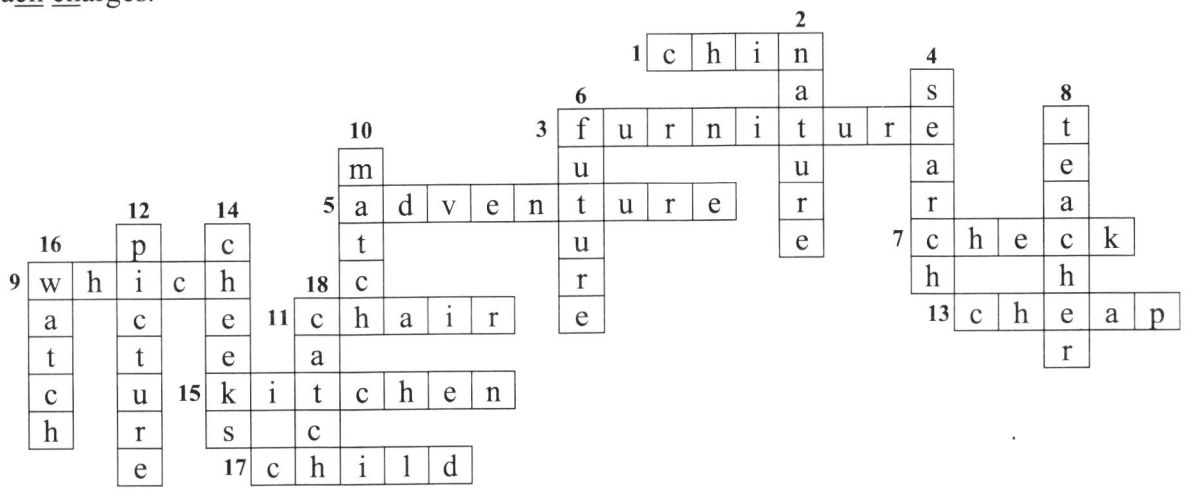

Consonant letter 'c' pronounced as /s/ as in cents, peace   Answers

The city celebrated twice in December with an exciting circus, and excellent dancing and racing. The second 'c' in **circus** is pronounced /k/

```
                    2           4
                    D   1 c  i  t  y
                    e      6 c
          3 m e d i c i n   e
                    e        i
                  5 m i c    e
              8*      b      e
        7 d e c i d e d        10
              e        r        d
      12      n      14 9 f a c e
      o    11 t w i c e       n
      f      e r      e        c
      f    16 r e   13 r i c e
      i      s        t
    15 c e l e b r a t e
      e      i        i
      c            17 o n c e
      e
```

*Note: The answer to **8 Down** can be 'center' (North American English spelling) or 'centre' (British English spelling).

Consonant letter 's'

His busy business is always noisy.

Words with the letter 's' pronounced as sound /s/	Words with the letter 's' pronounced as sound /z/
1) sad	1) refuse
2) song	2) was
3) sand	3) his
4) sat	4) busy
5) six	5) hers
6) second	6) does
7) stop	7) easy

Consonant letter 'g'

In the following words, the letter 'g' is pronounced with the sound /dʒ/.

The page about the gym had a general range of stages for gentlemen.

Words beginning with the letter 'g' pronounced as sound /g/	Words containing with the letter 'g' pronounced as sound /dʒ/ as in 'age'
1) go	1) gem
2) girl	2) general
3) gift	3) large
4) globe	4) gym
5) glass	5) strange
6) good	6) change
7) grapes	7) age

Consonant clusters at the beginning of words

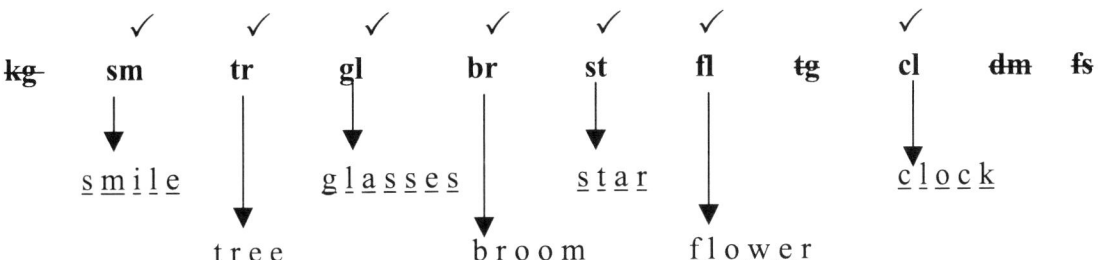

| ~~kg~~ | ✓ sm | ✓ tr | ✓ gl | ✓ br | ✓ st | ✓ fl | tg | ✓ cl | ~~dm~~ | fs |

s_m_i_l_e   g_l_a_s_s_e_s   s_t_a_r   c_l_o_c_k

t_r_e_e   b_r_o_o_m   f_l_o_w_e_r

Consonant clusters at the beginning of words: str, scr, spr

Words Down ↓   **Words Across** →

w	v	s	t	r	a	i	g	h	t	w	s	c	r	e	a	m	b
y	n	b	s	c	r	o	l	l	y	s	c	r	a	t	c	h	o
x	p	s	t	r	e	a	m	z	s	c	r	a	p	e	h	v	l
z	s	t	r	i	n	g	k	w	x	r	e	m	s	n	g	s	s
s	t	r	e	t	c	h	r	p	t	e	w	s	t	r	i	c	t
p	r	a	s	t	r	u	g	g	l	e	q	t	r	v	y	r	r
r	i	y	s	g	w	m	k	l	p	n	w	z	i	t	f	u	e
a	p	s	t	r	o	k	e	h	s	b	r	x	k	l	m	b	e
y	x	w	s	t	r	o	l	l	v	s	p	r	e	a	d	w	t
s	p	r	i	n	k	l	e	x	s	p	r	i	n	g	v	g	x

There are 24 words altogether beginning with either str, scr or spr

A dotted line ········ appears where words intersect across and down.

str		**scr**	**spr**
straight	strict	scrub	sprinkle
stream	string	scrape	spread
stray	strip	scratch	spring
street	strike	scream	spray
stress	stroke	screen	
stretch	stroll	screw	
	struggle	scroll	

Consonant clusters – words ending with the letters 'ld'   Answers

		k	g	p	s	
		t	o	l	d	
	c	j	l	n		
	o	l	d			
v	p	l	n			
b	a	l	d			

(crossword grid with letters: d u q f / w i l d / s h y l k / f i e l d / q k w l / s o l d)

1) This means the opposite to 'young' _ __old__

2) This describes someone without hair __bald__

3) This word means 'to construct' __build__

4) Past verb form of 'sell'. __sold__

5) Past verb form of 'hold' __held__

6) A place where sheep or cows eat grass. __field__

7) This means the opposite to 'hot'. __cold__

8) Past verb form of 'tell'. __told__

9) This word means 'in its natural state/not controlled' __wild__

10) This is a very valuable metal. __gold__

Consonant clusters – words ending with the letters 'st'

(crossword grid with letters: b u r s t / i n t e r e s t / g u e s t / c h e s t / w o r s t / p a s t / h o n e s t / i n s i s t / x t a s t e)

1) better than anything else __best__

2) a person who is invited __guest__

3) a written or spoken examination __test__

4) the time before the present time __past__

5) the opposite meaning to 'best' __worst__

6) A balloon will do this if you stick a pin in it. __burst__

7) the feeling of wanting to learn more about something __interest__

8) the front of the body below the neck, above the waist __chest__

9) to say strongly that something is true or must happen __insist__

10) to try some food to see if you like it __taste*__

11) the amount of money needed to buy something __cost__

12) This word describes someone who tells the truth. __honest__

13) an animal or insect that damages plants or food __pest__

14) to use too much of something or not use it carefully __waste*__

Note: 'taste' and 'waste' end in silent 'e' letters – the 'e' is not pronounced.

Consonant clusters – words ending with the letters 'nd' or 'nk'

The word 'thank' is listed twice.

```
                    t r e n d
                    t h i n k
                    h a n d
                    s a n d
                l i n k
              b a n k
            b l a n k
        r e s p o n d
        f r i e n d
```

1) a change or development in what is happening in society <u>trend</u>
2) You do this with your brain. <u>think</u>
3) This has four fingers and a thumb. <u>hand</u>
4) the final part of something <u>end</u>
5) the thick, outer skin of lemons and oranges <u>rind</u>
6) There is usually a lot of this at the beach. <u>sand</u>
7) to tell someone you are grateful for something they have done <u>thank</u>
8) to fall below the surface of the water <u>sink</u>
9) a connection between people, places or things <u>link</u>
10) an institution where you can keep or borrow money <u>bank</u>
11) a piece of paper which contains no writing or drawing <u>blank</u>
12) to say or do something as an answer to something <u>respond</u>
13) a person you know well and like <u>friend</u>
14) to arrive on the ground after travel by plane <u>land</u>
15) a small ground of people who play popular music <u>band</u>

Homophones (1) Answers

1) Please **write** your name in the **right** side of the page.
2) We'll have to **wait** for the trolley to help us lift such a heavy **weight**.
3) They're not sure **whether** the **weather** will improve by tomorrow morning.
4) They **rode** the tired horses along the dusty **road**.
5) I had a late breakfast of cooked **cerea**l and watched the exciting **serial** on TV.
6) I **resent** a copy of the most **recent** magazine as they said the previous copy didn't arrive.
7) The **principal** of the school said that the most important **principle** to remember was that, 'Honesty is the best policy'.
8) The **presence** of the police ensured that the stolen **presents** were returned to the correct address.
9) The building **site** was an ugly **sight** for the tourists.
10) I am so happy he's **passed** his driving test at last. He's done so much study and practice in the **past** few months.

Homophones (2) - Answers

1) When planting the young **berry** plants, make sure you **bury** the roots to the correct depth.

2) The sign says the audience is not **allowed** to sing **aloud** as they watch the musical concert.

3) The children **threw** the ball **through** the hole in the fence.

4) We **ate** a large meal at **eight** o' clock last night.

5) He is a **boarder** at an excellent school near the northern **border** of the country.

6) I can't **bear** to have my head **bare** in the extreme heat of summer – I must wear a hat.

7) The young boy wants a **real** fishing line and **reel** this summer, rather than the fishing net he used last summer.

8) He **tied** the little boat to the wooden post so it wouldn't float away with the strong **tide**.

9) We are **sure** we saw a large crocodile on the **shore** of the lake.

10) I'll have to **meet** you after I've bought the **meat** for dinner.

Homophones (3) - Answers

1) Have you **guessed** who the special **guest** at tonight's concert is going to be?

2) You won't have any **peace** until you give him another **piece** of the cake.

3) **Pour** some warm water over the **poor** injured dog's **paw**.

4) We could hear the tree branches **creak** as we walked along the side of the **creek**.

5) They are renewing the **coarse** surface of the golf **course** car park to make it smoother.

6) Did you **break** the glass of your rear **brake** lights when you had the car accident?

7) My husband is **sealing** the cracks in the **ceiling** before he paints it again.

8) He didn't tell me I had been walking around the **whole** day with a **hol**e in my trousers.

9) As soon as I saw the **new** dress, I **knew** I had to buy it.

10) Fortunately, the **plane** made an emergency landing on the flat, dusty **plain**.

Homophones (4)

1) The **rose**, being a very bright flower, looks best when it's planted in straight **rows**.

2) The **steel** bars were tied together so that nobody could **steal** them.

3) Have you noticed how everyone **stares** at her as she walks down the **stairs**.

4) The **stationary** bus blocked the sign above the entrance to the **stationery** store.

5) I **sent** my friend a card and a bottle of sweet smelling **scent** to make her feel better.

6) The accident **scene** was the most terrible thing I had ever **seen**.

7) This box is **too** heavy for **two** people **to** carry – we'll need at least three people.

8) I don't like to **waste** delicious food but I can't eat another thing – my **waist** is getting too big!

9) The hat suddenly **blew** off her head in the strong wind and floated across the **blue** water.

10) We **were** going to **wear** the same clothes to the party but we've changed our minds.

Note: The words **were** and **wear** are pronounced a little differently but the spelling of these words is often confused.

Pronouns - pronunciation and spelling in context   Answers

1) **His** camera was stolen while <u>he</u> was overseas last week, and **he's** still angry about it.

2) **We're** very happy with the results of <u>our</u> business trip. We visited over ten companies while we **were** overseas.

3) **You're** much taller than **your** brother but he's older than <u>you</u>, isn't he?

4) We have a new cat and **it's** sitting on the mat. **Its** name is Kitty and <u>it</u> eats a lot.

5) **Their** daughter has just graduated with excellent results, so **they're** very proud and happy. <u>They</u>'ve just been to the graduation ceremony.

Spelling in context (1)

The **twelve** underlined words contain the **correct** spelling.

Time and Change

It's <u>**right**</u> to say that life has changed. The pace and <u>**style**</u> of life today is not the same as it was in our grandparent's day. Science has changed the <u>**way**</u> of life in almost every place on earth at <u>**quite**</u> an amazing pace. I'm <u>**sure**</u> you can think of many changes that have occurred in your lifetime.

We now have machines that reduce work and make <u>**more**</u> free time available to relax each day. Science has developed ways to reduce crime and medicines to take away disease and <u>**pain**</u>. We can now travel <u>**great**</u> distances very quickly by <u>**plane**</u> or train, where people of the past had to allow a lot of time to walk, ride or <u>**sail**</u> to far away places. We can now communicate almost immediately by e-mail rather than waiting many <u>**days**</u> to receive letters by regular <u>**mail**</u>. Yes - it's impossible to deny that the pace and style of life has changed in many ways!

Spelling in context (2)

The **fourteen** underlined words contain the **correct** spelling.

Sport

From the earliest recorded history through to modern times, sporting events have **always** **been** popular. **Some** of the earliest known sports are still played today, but many of the details about how sport is played have changed. **For** example, in the past women **were** not **allowed** to play some types of sport. Also, some types of sport **were** only played by wealthy people.

In our modern times, sport can be enjoyed by **almost** everyone in society, **whether** they are rich or **poor**. Not everyone actually plays sport; however, many people who can't play, enjoy watching other people compete in **different** types of sport. Some people prefer indoor games such as table tennis or darts. Some prefer games such as tennis or squash that are played on a **court**. Other people enjoy very active sports such as soccer or hockey.

For many people, sport is their **main** form of entertainment and relaxation. On the other hand, there are people who are not interested in sport of any type and think that sport is a complete **waste** of time. What do you think about sport?

Spelling in context (3)

The **twenty** underlined words contain the **correct** spelling.

Health and Happiness

Good health is important to every person, yet many people don't take enough care of **their** health. Doctors agree that to **be** healthy, it's important to have a balanced life. For example, they say it's important to have a balance between work and rest and to get **regular** **exercise**.

However, I'm **sure** you'd agree that in our busy world, it's not always **easy** to get and keep **balance** in our lives. Due to financial problems, many people work long **hours**, leaving little time at the end of their busy **week** to spend with their family and **friends**. They eat quickly and don't get enough rest or relaxation and then their health suffers due **to** **too** much stress.

Interestingly, doctors now agree that having balance in **our** lives will bring, not only better health, but also a **greater** chance of **success**. If we can keep our lives more balanced, we will have **more** energy, and **reach** our goals in a more relaxed way; without feeling the **harmful** effects of stress in our **lives**.

The underlined words contain the **correct** spelling.

The Challenge of Learning a Language

Learning a new language can be a challenge. For example, when we hear people speaking an unfamiliar language, it **may be** difficult to hear **where** one word finishes and another word begins. The speakers sound as if **they're** speaking much **too** fast and **their** words sound as if they are all joined together into one very, very long sentence, without one **pause**.

This problem can be helped **by** understanding the difference between written and spoken language. **For** example, in *written* English, words can be seen with spaces between them on a page but in *spoken* English, words are **often** linked together and may be difficult to **hear** as separate words. For this reason, when beginning to learn a **new** language, it can be useful to **read** and listen to a text at the same time. This method helps learners to become familiar with the **way** speakers link words together.

A **useful** method for learning new words, is to try to guess the meaning of the words as you read **through** the text. When you have **read** the complete text, check your **dictionary** to **see** if you have **guessed** the meaning correctly.

Remember that learning to understand and speak a new language well doesn't usually happen quickly – it takes time, **patience** and a lot of **practice***.

*'**practice**' is the correct spelling for the <u>noun</u> form of this word in both American and British English. In British English, '**practise**' is the spelling for the <u>verb</u> form.

'Silent' syllables

When spoken at normal conversational speed, the syllables in brackets are often deleted in the following words.

1) int(e)resting
2) ev(e)ry
3) diff(e)rent
4) fam(i)ly
5) choc(o)late
6) bus(i)ness
7) sev(e)ral

8) cam(e)ra
9) ref(e)rence
10) sep(a)rate
11) comf(or)table
12) fact(o)ry
13) temp(e)rature
14) av(e)rage

Note: The final 'e' on *chocolate, reference, separate, comfortable, temperature, average* are always 'silent'.

Part 6 – Spelling Reference Lists – vowels

Ways of spelling the short vowel sound in the word **f<u>u</u>n**.
Write your dictionary symbol for this sound here _____

u	o	ou
s<u>u</u>ch	s<u>o</u>me	tr<u>ou</u>ble
c<u>u</u>lture	m<u>o</u>ney	c<u>ou</u>ntry
h<u>u</u>ngry	loves	y<u>ou</u>ng
b<u>u</u>tter	h<u>o</u>ney	

Less usual spelling: fl<u>oo</u>d

Ways of spelling the short vowel sound in **p<u>i</u>nk**.
Write your dictionary symbol for this sound here _____

i		y	u ui	e
c<u>i</u>ty	big	s<u>y</u>mbol	b<u>u</u>siness g<u>ui</u>lt	<u>E</u>nglish
ch<u>i</u>ldren	pink	gym	b<u>u</u>sy b<u>ui</u>lding	pr<u>e</u>tty
sit				
drink				
milk				
visit				

Note: The letter 'o' in the word 'w<u>o</u>men' is an exceptional way of spelling the sound /ɪ/.

Spelling Reference Lists – vowels

Ways of spelling the short vowel sound in the word **red**.
Write your dictionary symbol for this sound here _____

e		ue	ea	a
red		guess	ready	any
ten		guests	health	many
better			wealth	
less				
stress				

Less usual spelling: friend, bury, leopard

Ways of spelling the vowel sound in the word **stop**.
Write your dictionary symbol for this sound here _____

o	a
strong	want
long	quality
lost	wallet
shop	watch
got	
robbed	

Less usual spelling: knowledge, cough

Spelling Reference Lists – vowels

Ways of spelling the short vowel sound in the words **pull**.
Write your dictionary symbol for this sound here _____

u	oo	ou
p<u>u</u>ll	f<u>oo</u>t	w<u>ou</u>ld
p<u>u</u>sh	g<u>oo</u>d	c<u>ou</u>ld
p<u>u</u>t	c<u>oo</u>k	sh<u>ou</u>ld
f<u>u</u>ll	b<u>oo</u>k	
s<u>u</u>gar	c<u>oo</u>kie	

Less usual spelling: w<u>o</u>man

Ways of spelling the long vowel sound in the word **gr<u>ee</u>n**.
Write your dictionary symbol for this sound here _____

* A general rule when spelling this long sound is:
Put 'i' before 'e', except after 'c'.

ea	ee	e	ie*	ei*	'y' as word ending
l<u>ea</u>ve	s<u>ee</u>	th<u>e</u>se	p<u>ie</u>ce	rec<u>ei</u>pt	full<u>y</u>
r<u>ea</u>ch	t<u>ee</u>ns	<u>e</u>qual	th<u>ie</u>ves	rec<u>ei</u>ve	Also pronounced as a shorter sound in some varieties of English.
r<u>ea</u>son	gr<u>ee</u>n	sh<u>e</u>	bel<u>ie</u>ves	dec<u>ei</u>ved	
<u>ea</u>sy	ch<u>ee</u>se	h<u>e</u>			
	f<u>ee</u>ls				

Less usual spelling: mach<u>i</u>ne, p<u>eo</u>ple

Spelling Reference Lists – vowels

Ways of spelling the vowel sound in the word **s<u>oo</u>n**.
Write your dictionary symbol for this sound here _____

oo	u	o	ou	ew
c<u>oo</u>l	r<u>u</u>de	pr<u>o</u>ve	gr<u>ou</u>p	fl<u>ew</u>
sch<u>oo</u>l	r<u>u</u>les	m<u>o</u>ving	thr<u>ough</u>	gr<u>ew</u>
r<u>oo</u>ms	comp<u>u</u>ters	appr<u>o</u>ved		
s<u>oo</u>n				

Less usual spellings: fr<u>ui</u>t, sh<u>oe</u>

Ways of spelling the vowel sound in the word **p<u>ur</u>ple**.
Write your dictionary symbol for this sound here _____

i(r)	e(r)	o(r)	u(r)	ea(r)
b<u>ir</u>d	c<u>er</u>tain	w<u>or</u>d	t<u>ur</u>n	l<u>ear</u>n
f<u>ir</u>st	h<u>er</u>	w<u>or</u>st	n<u>ur</u>se	s<u>ear</u>ch
thirty	t<u>er</u>m	w<u>or</u>k	p<u>ur</u>ple	<u>ea</u>rly
girls				
skirts				

Less usual spelling: journey

Spelling Reference Lists - vowels

Ways of spelling the vowel sound in the word **sport**.
Write your dictionary symbol for this sound here _____

o(r	ou(r)	ar	* a aw au
form morning	course court	warm warned towards	call law caught
			*In words such as 'call', 'law', 'caught', some speakers of North American English pronounce the vowel sound /ɑ/.

Ways of spelling the vowel sound in the word **voice**.
Write your dictionary symbol for this sound here _____

oy	oi
employ destroy boy toys enjoyment	soil boil avoided noisy spoilt

Less usual spelling: lawyer

Spelling Reference Lists - vowels

Ways of spelling the vowel sound in the word **d<u>ay</u>**.
Write your dictionary symbol for this sound here _____

'a' with final silent 'e'	ay	ey	ai
r<u>ace</u>	d<u>ay</u>	ob<u>ey</u>	m<u>ai</u>n
c<u>ase</u>	alw<u>ay</u>s	th<u>ey</u>	compl<u>ai</u>n
s<u>ame</u>	st<u>ay</u>ed		w<u>ai</u>ted
pl<u>ace</u>	d<u>ay</u>s		tr<u>ai</u>n
l<u>ate</u>			

Less usual spelling: gr<u>ea</u>t, <u>ei</u>ght

Ways of spelling the vowel sound in the word **t<u>i</u>me**.
Write your dictionary symbol for this sound here _____

i	i + silent e	y	i + gh
child	time	why	fight
mind	hide	try	sigh
kind	like	flying	bright
	smile	sky	high
	nice		
	white		
	wine		
	lime		

Less usual spelling: <u>eye</u>, <u>ai</u>sle, g<u>ui</u>de, b<u>uy</u>

Spelling reference lists - vowels

Ways of spelling the vowel sound in the word **r<u>oa</u>d**.
Write your dictionary symbol for this sound here _____

o	o + silent 'e'	ow	oa
<u>o</u>nly	h<u>o</u>pe	kn<u>ow</u>	s<u>oa</u>p
w<u>o</u>n't	ph<u>o</u>ne	sh<u>ow</u>	c<u>oa</u>t
t<u>o</u>ld	wr<u>o</u>te	sn<u>ow</u>	r<u>oa</u>d
m<u>o</u>st	n<u>o</u>te	foll<u>ow</u>ed	c<u>oa</u>st

Less usual spelling: t<u>oe</u>, s<u>ew</u>, sh<u>ou</u>lder

Ways of spelling the vowel sound in the word **h<u>ou</u>se**.
Write your dictionary symbol for this sound here _____

ow	ou
p<u>ow</u>er	gr<u>ou</u>nd
n<u>ow</u>	c<u>ou</u>nt
br<u>ow</u>n	th<u>ou</u>sand
c<u>ow</u>s	m<u>ou</u>ntains
t<u>ow</u>n	s<u>ou</u>th

Spelling Reference Lists - Consonants

Words with 'silent' consonants

silent **w**	silent **k**	silent **h**	silent **g**	silent **b**	silent **l**
write	knee	hour	sign	climb	walk

Consonant sounds with more than one spelling pattern are included in the following lists

Ways of spelling the consonant sound in the word **f**unny, **ph**one, lau**gh**.
Write your dictionary symbol for this sound here _____

f	ph	gh
father	telephone	enough
fill	graph	laughed
found	elephant	cough
fixing		

Spelling Reference Lists

Ways of spelling the consonant sound in the word **ship, sure, action**.
Write your dictionary symbol for this sound here _____

sh	s	ss	ti
ship	sugar	passion	nation
short	sure	discussion	station

Less usual spelling: ocean, special, machine

Ways of spelling the consonant sound in the word **match**.
Write your dictionary symbol for this sound here _____

ch	tch	t
teach	watch	nature
chair	catch	adventure
check	butcher	future
which	kitchen	
cheap		
much		
each		
charges		

Other words to remember:

Spelling Reference Lists
Other words to remember:

Part 7 Reference Pages

Information about English verbs and irregular spelling

The letters **ed** are added to most verbs to form a past participle or past simple tense. eg. work →work**ed**. However, for some verbs, the spelling is *irregular* (doesn't follow the usual rules). eg. see → saw → seen. Look at the following examples:

A List of some Irregular Verbs:

base verb infinitive present simple	past simple	past participle for the present perfect tense use with *have/has*
be/am/is/are	was/were	been
beat	beat	beaten
become	became	become
begin	began	begun
bend	bent	bent
bite	bit	bitten
blow	blew	blown
break	broke	broken
bring	brought	brought
build	built	built
burn	burnt/burned	burnt/burned
buy	bought	bought
catch	caught	caught
choose	chose	chosen
come	came	come
dig	dug	dug
do	did	done
draw	drew	drawn
drink	drank	drunk
drive	drove	driven
eat	ate	eaten
fall	fell	fallen
feed	fed	fed
feel	felt	felt
fight	fought	fought
find	found	found
fly	flew	flown
forget	forgot	forgotten
forgive	forgave	forgiven
get	got	got/gotten
give	gave	given
go	went	gone
grow	grew	grown
have	had	had
hear	heard	heard
hide	hid	hidden
hold	held	held
keep	kept	kept
know	knew	known
lay	laid	laid
lead	led	led
leave	left	left

base verb infinitive present simple	past simple	past participle for the present perfect tense use with *have/has*
lend	lent	lent
light	lit	lit
lose	lost	lost
make	made	made
mean	meant	meant
meet	met	met
pay	paid	paid
read /ri:d/	read /red/	read /red/
ride	rode	ridden
ring	rang	rung
rise	rose	risen
run	ran	run
say	said	said
see	saw	seen
sell	sold	sold
send	sent	sent
show	showed	shown
sing	sang	sung
sit	sat	sat
sleep	slept	slept
speak	spoke	spoken
spell	spelt	spelt
spend	spent	spent
spring	sprang	sprung
stand	stood	stood
steal	stole	stolen
sting	stung	stung
swear	swore	sworn
swim	swam	swum
swing	swung	swung
take	took	taken
teach	taught	taught
tear /teər/	tore	torn
tell	told	told
think	thought	thought
throw	threw	thrown
understand	understood	understood
wake	woke	woken
wear	wore	worn
win	won	won
write	wrote	written

SPELL

Reference Page – American and British Spelling

Below are some example of common differences between British and American spelling.

British English

re ending

centre

litre

metre

theatre

single '1'

enrol

fulfil

our

colour

favourite

flavour

harbour

honour

labour

neighbour

Other differences

licence (noun)

practise (verb)

aluminium

catalogue

cheque

programme

tyre

American English

er ending

center

liter

meter

theater

double 'll'

enroll

fulfill

or

color

favorite

flavor

harbor

honor

labor

neighbor

license (noun and verb)

practice (noun and verb)

aluminum

catalog

check

program

tire

Phonemic Chart of English Sounds

The phonemic symbols displayed below and used in this resource are the ones used in many modern dictionaries and English language course books and are based on the International Phonetic Alphabet of English sounds.

Below each sound symbol are examples of words containing the sound.

Vowel sounds

æ (short sound)	e (short sound)	ɒ (not used in USA)	ə (unstressed sound)
bl**a**ck h**a**t	r**e**d h**ea**d	h**o**t sp**o**ts	oth**er** broth**er**
ɑː (long sound)	ʊ (short sound)	ʌ (short sound)	ɪ (short sound)
*d**ar**k st**ar**s	g**oo**d b**oo**k	f**u**n r**u**n	th**i**nk p**i**nk
ɜː (long sound)	uː (long sound)	ɔː (long sound)	iː (long sound)
*p**ur**ple	bl**ue** m**oo**n	*f**our** m**ore**	gr**ee**n tr**ee**s

As the pronunciation of some English vowel sounds varies across and within countries, the example words are intended as a *general* guide.

Diphthong (two vowel) sounds

eɪ	ɔɪ	əʊ (also oʊ)	ɪə
gr**ey** d**ay**	b**oy** v**oi**ce	yell**ow** g**ol**d	cl**ear** b**ee**r
eə (also ɛə)	aɪ	ʊə	aʊ
f**ai**r h**ai**r	br**igh**t l**i**me	t**our** (also /tʊr/)	br**ow**n m**ou**se

Consonant sounds

Note: voiceless sounds are shown in a shaded box.

p	b	t	d
pet **p**ig	**b**ig **b**ag	**t**ell **t**wo	**d**irty **d**og
tʃ	dʒ	k	g
Chinese **ch**ild	**j**ust **j**oking	**k**eep **c**ool	**g**ood **g**irl
f	v	θ	ð
fill **f**our	**v**ery **v**ivid	**th**ink **th**in	o**th**er bro**th**er
s	z	ʃ	ʒ
sad **s**ong	**z**ig-**z**ag	**sh**ort **sh**eep	mea**s**ure A**s**ia
m	n	ŋ	h
milk **m**an	**n**o **n**ever	lo**ng** so**ng**	**h**ot **h**ill
l	r	w	j
little **l**ine	**r**aw **r**ice	**w**et **w**inter	**y**es **y**ou

*Note: In some varieties of English, the letter 'r' is clearly pronounced wherever it occurs in words, (eg. st**ar**, p**ur**ple, f**our**), however in some varieties of English, 'r' is only pronounced when it is followed by a vowel sound.

© Boyer Educational Resources, 2003

Did you borrow this book?
To order your own copy, check our web site for the supplier most convenient for you.

THIS TITLE	**ISBN (ordering number)**
Spelling and Pronunciation for English Language Learners	**1877074 04 7**

Would you like more practice with English pronunciation?

Would you like to <u>hear</u> the pronunciation of new words?

Would you like to become more confident in listening and speaking in English?

Using '***Understanding English Pronunciation – an integrated practice course***', along with its accompanying audio recording, you will:

- learn ways of overcoming listening and pronunciation problems

- hear extended stretches of speech which demonstrate features of spoken English

- examine the link between English spelling and pronunciation

- feel increasing confidence as your listening and speaking skills improve.

See details below:

TITLE	ISBN
Understanding English Pronunciation - an integrated practice course - Student Book	0 9585395 7 X
Understanding English Pronunciation - audio cassettes (set of 2)	0 9585395 8 8
Understanding English Pronunciation - audio CDs (set of 3)	1 877074 03 9
Understanding English Pronunciation - an integrated practice course - Teacher's Book	0 9585395 9 6

To order any of these resources, check our web site for the supplier most convenient for you.

Web site:	**Phone/fax:**	**E-mail:**
www.boyereducation.com.au	**+ 61 247 391538**	**boyer@emunet.com.au**